WORDS ON MUSIC

Ernst Bacon

GREENWOOD PRESS, PUBLISHERS
WESTPORT, CONNECTICUT

The Library of Congress has catalogued this publication as follows:

Library of Congress Cataloging in Publication Data

Bacon, Ernst, 1898-
   Words on music.

   1. Music--Addresses, essays, lectures. I. Title.
[ML60.B13W7 1973]   780   73-427
ISBN 0-8371-6768-X

Originally published in 1960
by Syracuse University Press, Syracuse, New York

Reprinted with the permission
of Syracuse University Press

First Greenwood Reprinting 1973

Library of Congress Catalogue Card Number 73-427

ISBN 0-8371-6768-X

Printed in the United States of America

For the opportunity and assistance needed for the completion of his manuscript, the author wishes gratefully to acknowledge his indebtedness to

Mr. Huntington Hartford
and
Chancellor William P. Tolley, Syracuse University

CONTENTS

The Teacher

Music and Society

Briefly Said

WORDS ON MUSIC

Introduction

This book deals with some of the less obvious aspects of present-day music in America. The public has little knowledge of what goes on behind the proscenium of concerts, operas, and broadcasts, or how fashions or reputations are made, and it seldom sees the need to appraise the merits of men in high places. Our professional music has long been a one-party affair. In its politics there is no organized opposition, though the scattered elements of resistance could well constitute a large majority of the profession. As to what I call the political side of the art (by which I mean its manner of being manipulated and not its connection with the machinery of state), enough will be said in this book to make the point clear.

While education is now undergoing a worried scrutiny, with resonance added by some of our international pollsters and prognosticators, almost nothing is said in criticism of our large orchestras, opera houses, college music schools, recording companies, concert bureaus, movies, broadcasters, and publishers, which certainly play a large part in the national education, and which add up to what has been estimated to be the fifth national industry, filling a willing, or unwilling, commensurate portion of our everyday lives. It is true that now and then a book is vaunted for its

3

disclosures of music's real life backstage; and, indeed, if a person cared to read between the lines, enough has been printed to cause him to reason that there is more that awaits telling. However, to borrow an expression that Theodore Roosevelt applied to President Taft, the authors mostly "mean well, but say it feebly." When not damning with faint praise, they praise with faint damns.

Not that this book pursues any particularly bold or courageous line. I have neither the gift nor the resources to be a reformer, statistician, muck-raker, racket-buster, or even gadfly. While I do bring out a few circumstances of which the profession is as much aware as the public is ignorant, it is nevertheless my main task to speak of attitudes rather than statistics.

It is awkward to dwell on the faults of so glamorized and well-dressed a business as music. To do so, however, one should at least have some point of reference, some basis of comparison in making a criticism. My vantage point lies somewhere between the American concept of citizenship and the experience we have enjoyed in American letters, which is the only mature art we possess.

Nothing is gained when the wish to have "arrived" is confused with the doubtful fact. We need only observe that in exchange for foreign artists and orchestras we have been sending abroad our own, led by Americans in citizenship only, and programming (rightly or wrongly) as few genuine American works as they do at home. Europeans, enjoying and praising our orchestras and artists, are again convinced that we are better at buying talent than at building it. This is not to say that individuals have not "arrived" in America: only that the nation as a whole has not achieved a proper level of musical self-respect, and lacking this it can hardly expect to win the unqualified admiration of others. The American musician does not sit easily in the saddle of authority and responsibility. The horse may be as much at fault as the rider.

If it were possible to sum up what stands most in the way of our musical self-realization, I would say it is centralization. This growing evil has indeed infected Europe of late, but in lesser degree and at a stage of less vulnerability. It is odd how few people realize that the nation's music is ruled from one little half a square mile of Manhattan: management, radio, recording, the union, criticism, publication, and even to some extent scholarship. This tyranny, even though it often pictures itself as benevolent, is in effect repressive to regionalism, restrictive to individualism, and destructive to aspiration. New York is not only a national market. It is a world market. If only the great centers abroad were similarly neutral as regards their musicians, then a proper state of reciprocity might prevail. But they are not, and as a result we are harboring an ill-balanced anationalism that dispirits no less than its purblind opposite excludes. There has been some amelioration of this fault of late, but not as much as is deduced from a few native concessions which remain the exception rather than the rule.

Posing the problem, I offer no simple remedy. An inferiority complex is not cured with a capsule. Walt Whitman said: "Produce great persons; the rest follows." But then one can't put a Sequoia seed into a tin can and expect much to happen. I have as high an opinion of American talent and vitality, as I have a low opinion of how it is treated. This is the essence of what I have to say.

THE PERFORMER

No more than any other talent is that for music
susceptible of complete enjoyment where there
is no second party to appreciate its exercise.

EDGAR ALLAN POE

Sometimes, looking at a score, I say to myself, "What marvellous music. But I must make it so."

PABLO CASALS

The Interpretive Art

People have a way of speaking more and more of "creativity" the less there is of it. In olden times every musician "made" music, just as today we expect a painter to paint his own pictures. There was no mystery about it. The average musical child (and that is by no means a minority) makes up tunes as soon as he learns to speak. We usually put a stop to that, unhappily, by throwing the instrumental classics at him and frightening him with their complex notation. If we just let him sing awhile, he might do something as pretty as he does with paints when intelligently left alone. Instead, too often we tend to discourage the inventive strain; then later, after it has been chased out of the house, we make an exalted mystery of it. Creativity needs but little promoting, yet a good deal of *allowing*. No one thinks of planting a seedling in a solid bed of manure; but a certain amount of weeding, cultivating, and even manuring are presently necessary, once the plant has started. This simple garden formula ought to suffice us; but instead, we prefer to educate our musicians in hothouses. So we go in for exotic plants, and our greatest pride is to raise musical orchids and papayas in places like Michigan or Ohio, where apples and corn (yes, corn!) would grow so handsomely.

But all the concern over "the composer" (most of all, the

9

"American composer," the very emphasis upon whom is an admission of his low station) becomes a perennial bore. It has a note of unreality, if not of condescension. Composers are not to be expected in droves. Our music schools should temper their efforts to swell the ranks of a profession that has so small a place in modern society. The composer should be an intellectual aristocrat, as he has been in the past, whatever his economic station. *An average artist is no artist at all.* At best he is an artisan. If he is encouraged to believe himself a composer for no better reason than that he can spell out a little counterpoint, or juggle around a twelve-tone row (which are about as difficult to learn as elementary sentence structure or long division), then we cannot be surprised at the public's bewilderment at the results. An artist need not be a Beethoven or a Michelangelo, as some persons seem to insist, but he ought early to respect such towering genius, which in itself is already a promise of distinction. He is not properly in competition with other artists, but is never out of *competition with himself.* He strives to equal his own capacities, and this is no average assignment.

Now, in our better circles we have been saying so much about the composer, and forgetting that once he was synonymous with the musician. I doubt if anyone called Bach a composer in his day. But he was widely known as an organist. A musician of that time played, wrote, directed and taught. If we imagine that our age of specialization, or "expertness," produces better players, writers, conductors, and teachers, because of their narrowed fields, we are mistaken. Art has not become more complex, nor more highly organized, as have science and industry. On the contrary, it is today in many respects simpler, lesser in scale and notably less fecund. The output of a Stravinsky or a Hindemith (to name the most prolific) is small beside that of an Alessandro Scarlatti or a Handel. No modern oratorio measures in size, organization and complexity with the *St. Matthew Passion,* nor has an opera of the dimensions of *The Ring* been conceived since Wagner. No one today paints murals of the size and complexity of Tintoretto's or Rubens'.

The specialization of today exists not because of artistic needs, but is imposed from outside by business, which takes its cue from industry and sports. Business wants "production" in the sense of repetition (repetition and reputation, as Manuel Komroff remarked, have a close bond). It wants champions too. But the decathlon is not in its repertory.

And yet, the great composers of the past, like Bach, Handel, Mozart, Beethoven, Wagner, Mendelssohn, Liszt, and Chopin, were at once the great interpreters, and often the great teachers too, for it transpired that every one of their activities fed into every other. Conducting and piano, or organ playing, were replete with the experience of writing; writing was full of the experience of performing; and both were usually tempered through teaching. But this was not our modern teaching, per se; it was an *apprenticeship*, in which the student accompanied the master in his labors of construction, instead of learning an academic manual of arms in the ranks of a classroom.[1] The main object was always *to do* and the student learned by doing. There was none of the tendency, which prevails in most of our modern schools and against which Leonardo warned, of allowing "theory to outstrip performance." The old masters taught by the best of all precepts: example. Their words were loaded with deeds. In contrast, our colleges expect so much talk that art soon, as Wilde put it, "explains itself away," all poetry being reduced to prose, all instinct bogging down in intellect.

Even in our own day we have seen a few of these grand old versatile fellows who were at home in all of music: Rachmaninoff, Strauss, Tovey, Casals, Enesco, and Kreisler. They wrote, played, conducted, and mostly were masters of more than one instrument. Could anyone deny the richness and breadth of their interpretations of the classics, beside those of the specialized acrobat

---

[1] If a composer today were to put his students to work copying off the parts of a new score, I dare say there would be a great outcry about "exploitation." But we know that Bach's students all did this; and indeed, what better way is there to learn instrumental idioms and ranges, acquire accuracy and precision and learn the style of a chosen master? Mr. Roy Harris is one of the few writers today who has successfully revived this admirable practice.

virtuosos? But even they were forced, at least to the public eye, into specialization in order to prove their first-rateness, and to justify their inclusion in the "stables" of concert managers. Had any one of them extended his field of public enterprise beyond his advertised specialty, he would have gained not a new following, but lost instead much of his old.

If we look for American national music (and I believe it is worth looking for, provided we do not make a great noise about it), we make a mistake when we emphasize nationalism in any one branch of the art alone, and leave out the others. The composer, the critic, the conductor, the singer, the instrumentalist, the teacher are each a part of the picture. If we want to help the composer, we had best support those of our conductors and soloists who will perform his work. If we want to help the pianist, we should encourage the composer who will give him something special and new to perform. If we want to help the teacher, we should provide his students with professional outlets in concert and opera, something better to look forward to than only the academic treadmill. If we want to help the native conductor, then our critics should speak up for his right to compete fairly for conducting posts. If we want to help the critic, we should provide him with something better to write about than Maestro X's latest assault on the Brahms *First*.

I have always hoped for a place where all the elements needed for creative and interpretive music could foregather toward a national art, which in its very nationality would achieve an international appeal, and lend us stature abroad as well. This is the more important at a time when our political nationalism has aroused so much misunderstanding, and even mistrust, in foreign lands. Such a place has yet to be found or made. It could learn from the Florence of Boccaccio, the Weimar of Goethe, the Vienna of Mahler, the Dublin of Yeats, the Concord of Emerson, the Chapel Hill of Paul Green and Koch, not to forget the Leipzig of Mendelssohn. So far, neither Tanglewood, nor Aspen, nor any of the larger festivals and centers, despite their undoubted excellence, have quite achieved this. For they are still postulated on a certain degree of American inferiority, and they operate in a vacation milieu.

In a way, a performance is in itself no less than a creation in that it resurrects a mere record of another's thought. "What is necessary," says Casals, "is to bring to life what is written." And it takes every bit as much labor and thought to recreate as to create. It happens that one is often more conscientious about learning a classic than about writing a new work. A sonata is usually written in a matter of months, sometimes weeks. But the pianist may study the *Appassionata,* or an actor may study *Lear,* for a lifetime, and still not feel satisfied with the result. Strauss was known at times to have speeded up his tempi when conducting his own operas for fear of delaying his midnight game of Skat; but he never consulted his watch while directing Mozart. Toscanini, after leaving an incomparable record of performances, is said to have busied himself after retirement with the Beethoven scores, hoping to explore yet deeper their inner secrets.

Doubtless, each generation will have to restudy these same classical works with reference to its own time. The Toscanini recordings of Wagner, possibly the best of our time, may prove inadequate for another day. Indeed, it was he who demonstrated in Bayreuth that the traditions handed down from Wagner regarding his own operas had become mostly obsolete, coining the famous apothegm, that "tradition is laziness." Toscanini made these operas live *for our time* and not Wagner's. Likewise the definitive recordings of today's performances may in turn become the period-pieces of tomorrow. But there will probably remain, as in certain creations, a few interpretations that will continue to be valid over long periods because of their quality of truth and insight. Shakespeare left no tempo indications nor dynamic marks to help the actor (not even stage directions); yet we may well doubt whether the plays have suffered because each new generation is obliged to find its own way with them, and there are no "authentic" records of performance to lean on.

The effort to bring to life a work of the past is immensely rewarding. The danger lies in the convenience and availability of recordings. It is so easy to listen to another's performance on a record; and no less easy to fall into the habit of imitating it, and accepting it as authoritative. Who are you to dispute what Victor or Columbia have chosen as definitive? We can forgive and even sometimes approve students learning by imitation from records, but what will we say to famous concert artists doing this? And yet there is discoverable a revealing likeness between many of those recordings that are offered us as new and individual revelations of interpretation.

One thing to notice is the ever growing *correctness* of the records, which shows that a good deal of patching has gone on behind the scenes, for we know that live performances are seldom so accurate. Correctness is not perfection, and is no proper substitute for what the Germans call *Zug* (which is something between impulse and spontaneity).

It is this spontaneity that is often lost during the process of recording. For there is nothing, not even the stimulus of a studio audience, that can free an artist wholly from the anxious realization that the microphone picks up every least defect in his performance. If a defect, however small, is left in the record, it will be magnified into a blemish with every repetition by the eventual listener, who will see or partake of none of the gesture or occasion that accompanied, and perhaps even justified, its occurrence. The conscientious record-maker will therefore insert, for every imperfection, another playing of the same passage, which can never have quite the same proportions, since it is out of the context of the initial performance. But what is mainly lost is the daring and verve of a great presentation, the first condition for which is a live and responsive audience. The player must be free. Improvisation has already long disappeared from our concerts (in which so much money is invested that nobody can afford risks). With recording, the risk becomes unthinkable.

The phonograph shares with musicology the distinction of having made America more literate in music. Not overlooking some exceptions where it has stimulated hitherto neglected fields (like chamber music), the phonograph has also become a substitute for the concert, just as the cinema has supplanted the theatre, yet without adding, like the cinema, a new art of its own.

But to return to the problem of recordings. Until their advent, the composer enjoyed some solace from the realization of his declining prestige by comparison with the performer in the assurance that his work had a chance of enduring. Today it is the virtuoso whose voice is given permanent form through the tape and the disk. The writer, faced with a decreasing program of publication, and being fairly well ruled out of recording, as against the whole galaxy of masters of the past, is in a fair way to being the man facing oblivion with his works. Recording has reversed matters. Leonardo's idea that artists must produce for the ages is out of fashion. The performer now enjoys posterity.

Within the framework of the classical amenities and without violating a single canon of taste, an interpreter has all the room he needs to be himself. It is no accident that some great creative men were torn from their marriage with creation by that siren, performance: Liszt, Mahler, Rachmaninoff, and Paganini. "When Rubinstein [Anton, of course] plays to us the *Sonata Appassionata* of Beethoven, he gives us not merely Beethoven," said Oscar Wilde, "but also himself . . . Beethoven made vivid and wonderful to us by a new and intense personality. . . . In point of fact, there is no such thing as Shakespeare's Hamlet. . . . There are as many Hamlets as there are melancholies."

The public will finally sense what the artist has put into his work. It is almost axiomatic that *the listener will feel what the performer feels*, though it sometimes happens that a feeling becomes so well embodied in the performer's habit that in the very routine of repetition it appears to be present even after it is lost. It follows then that the more the player sharpens the listener's attention, the more he himself is obliged to maintain a level of sharp concentration. The careless player, on the other hand, who holds only half the listener's attention, has little to fear from his imperfections. They will pass unnoticed; but so will the music. It is strange how well the public senses how close the artist has come to this realization of himself, and values him accordingly.

*Do not saw the air too much with your hand,
but use all gently; for in the very torrent, tem-
pest and, as I may say, the whirlwind of passion, you must acquire and beget a temperance
that may give it smoothness.*

WILLIAM SHAKESPEARE

The Podium

A Navaho Indian had been prevailed upon to attend a symphony concert at which Alfred Hertz conducted. On being introduced afterward to the conductor, he proffered the compliment: "I enjoyed the dance."

The notion that orchestral music is written so that conductors may caper, is not altogether strange. It may have prompted Professor Luening's wry proposal of a *concerto for conductor*. While it is true that conducting is a kind of dance and that a conductor should try to free himself of restraint in his physical exhortation to his players, there are limits to what he may allow himself, prescribed by his function as a leader and teacher, which is to make the orchestra play its best. This it will obviously not do, if it feels he is "showing off"—that is to say, if he is using the music to display himself rather than employing himself for the sake of the music.

The better players in an orchestra have all developed a style and taste that are more or less personal. Bowing, phrasing, the quality of tone, the vibrato, all proportions, are different for each individual. The daily and continued subordination of these facets of individuality to the teamwork required for a good orchestral ensemble can be achieved without artistic violence only by a

16

conductor whose artistry, knowledge, and tact are respected. A man's violin playing is virtually *himself* and the more it is so, the better artist he is. If he must yield this up, it should be to one who is his musical superior.

Contrariwise, an orchestra's unrelieved submission to the authority of an inferior, inconsiderate, or vulgar conductor, can make of this relation an unrelieved vice. The display-loving public, having not yet learned that the superior technique is that which is least in evidence, is inclined to encourage ostentation, and conspires thereby unwittingly to the further enthrallment of symphony players. It revels in the display furnished by the martinet, who makes it appear that the most miraculous effects of sound emanate from nothing more than a flick of the baton (or better still, the batonless hand), and who leans into a solo passage as if the players were ready to burst blood vessels for him. It loves the military fustian of the concerted movements of the strings (which in itself is proper enough). It marvels at the conductor's capacity to retain an entire score in memory.[1] It is no wonder then that a conductor sometimes suggests Aesop's fly sitting on the axletree of a chariot wheel who says, "What a dust do I raise." Or that the audience forgets who is the author of a symphony in its frenzied admiration for the maestro. Or again that the orchestral players may think, as Strauss' father, a hornist in the Munich Court theatre, expressed it: "Oh you conductors: you flatter yourselves about the miracle of your authority. Yet the moment you take over . . . the way you ascend the podium, open the score . . . before you have lifted the baton . . . we already know whether you are master or we."

Consider, then, the effect of a mediocre leadership on the art-life of a community that takes its weekly musical sermon in the

---

[1] Not to belittle the art and labor of memorizing a score (in some cases, as with Mitropoulos, down to the littlest detail), the public exhibits an inordinate wonder at the scoreless performance, not realizing that the orchestra has its music before it and will continue to play regardless of any possible memory slips of the conductor. Should a conductor be vague in his recollection of a cue, he need only glance up, to catch an anticipatory gesture in the players. Eugene Goossens, being once asked why he, too, did not follow the prevalent fashion of conducting without score, replied: "The answer is simple: I can read."

orchestra's hall, and the effect on composers and soloists. For, as Berlioz says: "A bad singer can spoil only his own part, while an incapable or malevolent conductor ruins all. The most admirable orchestra is then paralyzed, the most excellent singers are perplexed and rendered dull; there is no longer any vigor and unity; under such direction the noblest daring of the author appears extravagance; inspiration is violently brought down to earth."

The manipulation of a keyboard of black and white keys by a pianist is considered a respectable mastery. But to the uninitiate spectator the control over eighty-eight professional players seems ever so much more difficult than the mastery of eighty-eight keys. The comparison, however, is illusory. "It is harder to awake emotions in ivory keys," said Paderewski, "than it is in human beings." Indeed, it could be asked whether anyone should even have the right to step before such an august body of mature and accomplished players as a professional orchestra before having shown the fullest credentials of artist and musical officer (aside from those obvious technical requirements that go with orchestra direction, a full command of at least one instrument, a full mastery of score-reading, a comprehensive knowledge of the musical literature, and the relatively uncomplicated baton technique). How should he understand the right proportioning of a symphony, if he has never even learned to perfect and shape up a piano or violin sonata? And yet, today, a number of orchestral directors of prominence are persons whose careers as conductors date from the very moment of realization of their insufficiency as pianists, violinists, composers, or organists. With but little talent and learning in this demanding field, they discover in themselves an aptitude for the trivia of high social life, a leaning toward first-rate tailors, and a passion for conspicuous ascendancy over their artistic superiors.

Instead, professional conducting should be the one field of music where a consummate mastery should be a condition *sine qua non*. Not that a conductor has not always more to learn. But he should not be allowed to acquire the rudiments of his art at the expense of professionals, as so many have been allowed or encouraged to do.

There is a story about the Chicago Orchestra, which, while on tour, was rehearsing *The Messiah* in a small midwestern town that had decided to blow itself to a famous orchestra for its annual choral concert. The local conductor, forgetting the unwritten law that he should confine his criticisms to the chorus, stopped the music twice to criticize the melodic playing of the cellos. Nothing happened, beyond a few added scrapings of the bow, until he repeated his admonition a third time, whereupon a venerable German cellist rose from the rear of the section and said, "Say Misterr, vun more vord from you, und donight ve follow you."

As in politics, a conductor should know when to lead and when to follow, when to command, when to yield. Nothing is more exasperating to an orchestra than a director who signalizes his authority at all times, fussy in anticipation of faults, and furious in their correction. An unrelieved exercise of compulsion is the surest sign of failure of the power of persuasion.

The tact of a leader shows itself in the avoidance of obvious and unnecessary directions. His knowledge of cues and other indications is often best shown by not giving them at all—of an eloquent musical statement, by *not* underscoring it. The orchestra soon senses his knowledge of the score, and despises an exhibition of this, whether to itself or the audience. His experience reveals itself in doing what is necessary and not a jot more. The rest of the time it is his business to go along with the music and to participate, however watchfully, in the enjoyment of the result. Nor is he entitled to make a public exhibition of his displeasure at his orchestra's shortcomings. He shares the responsibility for whatever happens, with the players. As well expect a pianist to make a wry face because of a mistuned string. The public is there to experience the music, and not to witness the maestro's hortative fury.

The conductor's beat is as necessary for himself as for the orchestra. Playing no instrument during a performance, it is his way of staying in rapport with the music. To control the rhythm *he must be in the rhythm.* He is pulled, and at times he must pull. The amplitude or character of the beat is a purely personal matter, and has little to do (barring downright ineptitude) with the orchestra's response. Ordinarily, the orchestra pays little attention to the hand or the stick. What the orchestra sees or feels is the intention. This is conveyed by the conductor's entire person. When a man is full of his music he forgets himself and his gesture. It is idle, therefore, to discuss the merits of large or small motions of direction, or of outward gestures, provided they are not offensive or interfering. The copious beat natural to one man becomes the affectation of another. All that is said about a conductor's "beat," or about his "left hand" is sheerest nonsense. What is often forgotten is that the real work is done in rehearsal (to which the public is rarely admitted). Furtwängler was asked, "What is the role of your left hand when you conduct?" To which he replied, "After over twenty years of conducting, I must say that I have never thought of it."

However deserving of respect and admiration an orchestra may be, its capacity for music-making is limited finally to the endowments of its conductor. The democratic relationships of chamber music cannot operate within so large a group, producing sounds of so heterogeneous and unequal a character. Early Soviet Russia, and later, New York, tried a conductorless orchestra. In both cases the direction was merely transferred from the advantageous position of the podium to the disadvantageous position of the first chair of the violins. Somebody had to start and stop the music, at least. As for interpretation, one might as well have expected strategy from an army ungeneraled. One wondered there was any balance at all; and the music mostly lost focus. The immediate remedy for a bad orchestra, then, is not to have *no* conductor at all, but to have a *good* conductor. The rest usually follows.

The beat and the gesture, like the speech and movement of an actor, can of course be studied. But they are not fully learned until they appear wholly unstudied. *The perfect technique obliterates itself.* It was a common experience, in watching Toscanini or Furtwängler, to feel that the art is after all very simple;

that anyone could easily do likewise. The summit of the interpretive art, as represented by great performers, consists in becoming the perfect vehicle of transmission. The mark of a great musical personality is the removal of his ego—the capacity to allow music to pass unhindered. Noninterference becomes the ultimate goal of study. It is a spiritual achievement. "The real task of the conductor," as Liszt said, "consists in making himself quite useless."

A great work greatly performed is a powerful spiritual force. A great work weakly performed is a profanation. The performer has a large responsibility. "The submissiveness and culture that we require of the creator," says Stravinsky, "we should quite justly and naturally require of the interpreter as well. For, I repeat, one *sees* music. An experienced eye follows, adjudges, sometimes unconsciously, the performer's least gesture."

The superior artist approaches a masterpiece with reverent trepidation. The inferior artist approaches it with bland confidence. The worst thing you can say of a conductor is to praise his beat, his gesture, his stern rule, his memory, or his left hand. The best thing to say is that it goes well with the music; that implies everything.

The Conductor as a Public Official

Our musical life has so developed that nearly all serious music revolves around the symphony orchestra. Some public money and a great deal of patronage go into its support. Most reputations are made through its performances, and indeed it alone, of all institutions, enjoys a full seasonal audience. Abroad, particularly in Germany and Italy, the opera and orchestra are mostly of equal importance. In larger European cities, the opera enjoys a season as long as the school year, and is largely supported from public funds. Vienna, Berlin, London, and Paris have at least two full-season operas each, the one more formal, the other more popular. The opera orchestras are, as often as not, the leading concert orchestras as well, as for example, the famous Vienna Philharmonic. In cities too small to support a full season of opera, it is customary to bring together under one roof both the musical and the nonmusical theatre. Plays and operas share the season. Every opera house has its own staff of conductors, principal and secondary singers, chorus, orchestra, stage director and crew. The "intendant" is the administrative head of the theatre, but the chief maestro usually wields an undisputed artistic authority. In the latter capacity were Mahler and Strauss in Vienna, Toscanini in Milan, Furtwängler in Berlin, Busch in Dresden. These men brought opera to its highest levels in modern times.

22

The symphony orchestra as the central institution for professional music is characteristic mainly of American cities. James Huneker remarked: "In the ultimate analysis it is the orchestra that most eloquently voices the musical ideals of our time . . . it is the profoundest interpreter of our profoundest ideas and feelings. It is the new church of an ancient and venerated religion, the religion of art." The conductor of the orchestra becomes thus the key personality, the unelected mayor, of the American musical community. Heading the only quasi-public-supported musical institution, he should certainly be looked upon as a public servant.[1] His responsibilities, therefore, go beyond giving concerts, rehearsing his orchestra, and entertaining his audiences; they extend to giving opportunity to the singers, instrumentalists, composers, teachers, and even conductors, of the locality, who have reached a point of artistry deserving the public recognition which only a symphony concert can give. His is a large assignment, and involves much more than just ordinary music-making. He gets paid for it, however, and his prestige is disproportionately large.

Nevertheless, few communities seem to be aware of what is involved. The selection of an orchestral leader is ordinarily left to a group of philanthropic citizens. Sometimes a single benefactor takes the entire initiative. However commendable the motive, it cannot be overlooked that the parties chiefly affected by the choice are rarely if at all consulted. They include: the regular subscription audience; the orchestra, whose professional existence and artistic life are at stake; and the professionals of the community, for whom the orchestra is the principal activating musical force. Rarely is such a post filled by open competition, or as the result of professional deliberation. The theory probably is that musicians are an undependable lot, inclined to jealousy and self-seeking, who should not be entrusted with such weighty matters, as if these traits were less in evidence among doctors,

[1] Public support is far from covering the deficits. In a few cities, San Francisco, Baltimore, and New York, and certain states, notably North Carolina and Vermont, there is a small subsidy from public funds. Otherwise it is endowments, as in Cleveland or Boston, or merely year-by-year guarantees, that support the orchestras.

politicians, lawyers, or educators. A patron giving a little money, or having a flair for making others do so, feels himself entitled then to settle at once the musical fate of a city for what may be an entire generation. For, once a conductor is engaged and he endears himself socially to patron circles, professional considerations will generally receive little notice. And yet it is well-nigh impossible for a city to rise above the musical level he sets, and the patrons are not likely to countenance rival organizations.

Meanwhile, the patron may be completely ignorant of music or musicians. If he (or she) does not already have in mind some favorite, he usually opens negotiations with a commanding New York concert management, which offers him a flattering invitation to join the big leagues, assuming he is not already there. This is tempting bait, but the Big Time ordinarily spells any orchestra which can achieve an annual deficit of a hundred thousand dollars or more. We have between twenty-five and thirty such at present. The possibility of emulating the Philadelphia orchestra is held out, through the engagement of some celebrated virtuoso conductor, the remoteness of whose origin has not a little to do with his presumptive qualifications. The patron has reason then to fancy himself the agent of an undertaking that promises, at one bound, to hurdle over all intermediate steps that stand in the way of the achievement of final perfection. Since he or his friends can afford it, *he prefers to buy what he has not the patience to build.*

Alfred Frankenstein, music and art critic of the *San Francisco Chronicle*, remarked: "The symphony orchestra or opera company which becomes a mere sounding board for big name 'artists' has been subverted from the purposes for which it was established and no longer deserves its economic shelter. There is the greatest possible confusion throughout our entire musical structure in regard to this matter, due not so much to evasion of responsibility as to failure to realize, define, delimit the responsibilities of each party to this complex. . . .

"Imagine a museum in which all acquisitions were made by a board none of whose members knew anything about art. Within six months it would be a junk shop of fake old masters, and it would never be anything else. The curator stands as buffer between the museum and dealer. He has not put the dealer out of business. He has merely put him in his place. The curator screens out what the market offers, according to its values, and he organizes the whole program of his institution according to the community's needs and potentialities.

"Our musical institutions on the other hand, are always run by boards of amateurs. The appeal of the merchant in this case is not to information and intelligence, but to ignorance, and especially to that widespread human failing which has been phrased by the Irish playwright in the line, ' 'Tis the far-off hills are green.' "

Delacroix once said, "Cold exactitude is not always art." True, an orchestra should be a kind of collective masterpiece, of a quality like a Steinway concert piano, or a Guarnerius violin. Certainly its presence is appropriate where there exists a congruous audience, capable of appreciating its qualities. No one quarrels with the high standard of the Philadelphia, Chicago, and New York "bands" (as the British say) in their own sophisticate environment. But in an area of unformed musical taste, the Boston Symphony would be as out of place as a Rolls Royce limousine on the Aleutian Islands. It would create a state of mutual embarrassment that could scarcely be conducive to a healthy musical development.

Mr. Hearst once thought it possible to transplant a European abbey to our shores. But to suppose that such an edifice could be the same here as there, merely because it is physically possible to dismember abroad, ship, and reassemble the building here, is to disregard its function, geographic situation, the prevailing climate, and the surrounding vegetation. It becomes an object of curiosity mainly. Rather than elevate taste, it invites contempt for native ingenuity. We travel to Europe to enjoy the architecture and those institutions of living that are so felicitously adapted to local environment. The beauty of an Alpine or an English village lies largely in its harmony with its surroundings. We go to be relieved of the disharmony and disorder that are left in the wake of our pioneering life and of the great wounds it has left on the landscape through the reckless exploitation of resources. Old Europe's lesson to us is one of propriety. (Is there anything to admire in the European imitation of our skyscrapers?)

Europeans look to us for vitality, opportunity, the fruits of a democracy, space, abundance, and freedom. But where will the American find these in his musical world? A man giving money should certainly be entitled to a voice in how it is used, but his should not be the only voice. We allow campaign contributions in politics, but we frown on evidences of their undue influence. And we need have no illusion that conducting is not politics in the fullest sense. The point is that, having recognized this, let us also expect of a conductor that he serve his community first and foremost, as even the humblest politician must expect to do. This is by no means assured, as things are today.

The initial task of a conductor is to create the best possible results with the means at hand: that is to say, with local men and their skills. He should exert himself first to bring the players of the area up to their own highest level of performance. If then after extended trials and instructions the results are unsatisfactory, he has the right to make the needed changes to achieve a better end. This requires patience and tact, and certain qualities of the teacher. If the players are made to feel that their artistic and physical livelihood depends mainly on the caprices and ambitions of their conductor, they cannot possibly do themselves full credit, and will be in constant fear of the axe falling on them. They will have to resort to entrenching themselves behind an organization interested not in artistic standards but only in wages and job security.[2]

---

[2] A union in music poses problems different from those in manufacturing. There is a distinction, often overlooked, between profitable enterprise, such as music for radio, television, movies, and dance, and costly, unprofitable enterprise such as symphony, opera, and sometimes publication. The provision for proper living standards by means of minimum wages and maximum working hours, arrived at through accepted methods of group action, is entirely feasible

An orchestra needs not always the finest players in order to give good performances. The interpretation of a work rests musically, if not technically, mainly with the conductor. A performance is not primarily, as with a string quartet, a composite of the participants' interpretations. *The orchestra is the conductor's instrument* just as a piano is the pianist's. Thus the old adage that there are no bad orchestras, only bad conductors.

The orchestra is at once the most splendid and the least democratic of musical institutions. An odd contradiction that it should have achieved its highest degree of technical regimentation in democratic America. Being then a kind of small musical army, the Napoleonic maxim, "Better an army of lambs led by one lion than an army of lions led by one lamb," could be translated to read: Better a good school band led by a Toscanini than the greatest orchestra led by some musical clod, or at best *routinier*. When people tell me Philadelphia, or any other city,

in the profit category, but may prove to be precarious, and even disastrous, where patronage and its concomitant, good will, are involved. A patron giving a sum of money to an orchestra, when faced with demands for more and a possible threat of strike, may well decide to withdraw his patronage entirely. Negotiations, however pressing their need may be, are of necessity delicate; they may not be pushed with the same inflexibility as in a teamsters' union. And yet the need for betterment of orchestral salaries is perennial and well-nigh axiomatic, calling once more for the attention of government in the face of a declining concentration of wealth among individual benefactors.

There is also another distinction, often lost sight of, between the *artisan* members of the union, who constitute the overwhelming majority of its membership, and the *artists*, who are in a very small minority, but who have been drawn into its ranks by virtue of its vertical organization. As would be expected, the highly educated artists have very little to say in matters of policy, and often find themselves immobilized, perhaps not by intention, but rather through the action of the rules laid down in behalf of the vast body of members (a quarter million), many of whom have no musical activity whatever. It is as if the entire business of the care of the sick were to be handled by one union, including nurses, superintendents, ambulance drivers, secretaries, orderlies, cooks, dishwashers, repair men and so forth. How then would the interests of the relatively few doctors be served? Clearly there is a conflict of interests here that warrants a restudy of objectives, if not a division of membership, so that all are properly served. It is not easy to find some common ground between those whose interests dictate they should give only what they must, and those who feel themselves impelled to give without limit, that is, the artists in the fullest sense of the word.

has the best orchestra, I ask, "Has it the best music?" It is like telling me Mrs. Jones has a fine collection of Strads. The point is, "Who plays them?"

In the lesser orchestras, of which there are many in this country, a conductor must reckon on spending the greater part of his time on organization. Most lesser orchestras are semiprofessional, in varying degree, and though this is desirable and proper, it produces many problems. There are the conflicting interests of union and nonunion players, and students. A money transaction, one way or the other, is usually necessary to assure proper attendance. Students *pay* for college credits and are obliged to attend rehearsals to receive them. Professionals, on the other hand, *are paid,* either to fill the unfilled spots in college orchestras; or else they themselves become the nucleus of civic orchestras. But when players neither pay nor are paid, they frequently incline to be lax in attendance and practice. To control these matters, and to enlist not only players but supporters, takes a great deal of painstaking labor, most of which falls on the conductor himself, partly because amateurs like to deal with the man at the head, and partly because there is seldom enough money to engage a full-time manager or assistant.

Quite often a successful organizer builds up a provincial orchestra which he has not the artistic talent later to carry beyond its formative stages of development. A conflict arises then between those who remain loyal to him in consideration of his labors, and those who want to make better music than that of which he is capable. In this dispute we often incline to be partial to the clever builder, and so the organizer wins out over the artist.

Conversely there is much great conducting talent lying dormant because its possessors are not given to doing the necessary organizing work. Abroad the support of operas and orchestras is largely traditional. The conductor works his way up the ladder, like any clerk in an already established institution. His labors are musical and seldom organizational. In this country we are in a formative stage as yet. It happens seldom that a conductor can escape the labors that go with putting an institution into motion. The talent for this has, of course, little correlation with musical talent, and as a result we by-pass some of our best potentialities.

The conductor of our large orchestras has come to have an enormous schedule of concerts, broadcasts and rehearsals—far more than anyone abroad, and more than should be allowed or expected of one man. Orchestras like Boston and Philadelphia may have over one hundred fifty concerts, broadcasts, and recording sessions a year. Our patrons expect their one maestro to do most of this, with the help perhaps of an assistant and an occasional guest conductor (who is usually engaged only by exchange and thus represents no relief of labor). The conductor is constrained to assent to this inhuman schedule, because he knows the alternative would be a division of authority and of salary. Management encourages this situation, finding it more profitable to exploit one overblown name than to deal with a number of names more fittingly proportioned to their possessors' respective abilities and accomplishments.

There is no reason to believe that the community is well served by this arrangement. A conductor carrying the burden of such an enormous season, not to mention his commitments abroad out of season, is of necessity far too busy and exhausted to give time to the examination of new talent, whatever his inclination may be. The pressure of decision forces him into choosing performers and works that have already passed muster in approved circles. The leisure to study and evaluate whatever is untried is not at hand. And so is the already exaggerated imbalance between the known and the unknown increased to even further extremes. Fame is a good deal like money; the two are very much in league. We accept the rule, if wryly, that "to them that have shall be given." But while our tax laws place limits to the acquisition of private wealth, there are no limits to the inequity of reputation. If our concept of citizenship is to include the right of musical talent to compete in the open market, then our orchestral system must be viewed as a feudal institution, the grandeur of which is bought at a high human price. Let it not be said (to paraphrase a famous line of Chinese poetry) that a conductor's reputation is built on a thousand artistic corpses.

Nor is the community well served by the unrelieved aspect of its maestro in concert throughout an entire season. However ably a man conducts, the public has a right to enjoy a variety of personalities performing on its orchestra. Certainly in all other fields of performance, including the opera, there is no comparable monopolization of musical resources. One would almost be led to think the orchestra is the conductor's private estate. There is a myth to the effect that an unchanging leadership improves an orchestra. No doubt one man can better impose his will upon a more or less defenseless group of others if he suffers no interruptions. But whether that will represents a good or a bad tendency remains a moot question. Orchestras may deteriorate no less than improve under such a discipline. Few people realize what contempt, possibly even hate, is engendered in an orchestra that must endure an inferior leader week in and week out, and even a good leader can become insufferable from the very lack of relief.

The ultimate question is, not how good is the orchestra; but rather how good is the music? And then, music, to be good, needs an audience, and that audience will be stimulated by every new personality on the podium. This does not say there should not be someone responsible for the orchestra's discipline and development. But his public appearances should be limited. Not only should every large orchestra employ a number of conductors, but there should be facilities allowing for touring conductors, just as for touring virtuosos. The complex of major American orchestras is sufficient to allow for many times the present number of conductors at small additional cost. Americans, conductors as well as audiences, should enjoy opportunity, variety, and enthusiasm, whereas now they have mainly frustration, monotony, and boredom.

This is the system worked out by management, where the agent no longer serves the artist but the artist has come to serve the agent. Let us suppose that an advertising agency were given the power to select and reject college presidents, army generals, surgeons, judges, and governors. Perhaps education, the military, medicine, the judiciary, and government would survive. But one would hardly expect any great developments to take place while these professions are enslaved to what must of necessity be a policy primarily of profit. A little business (to borrow from Herbert Spencer) is a good thing for art. But a business on such a vast scale is surely the sign of a misspent philanthropy.

All deep things are song, as if all the rest were wrappings and hulls.

THOMAS CARLYLE

The Singer

Until recent years composers have all written songs at some time, whether the song be called madrigal or minnelied, aria or chanson, melody or recitative, lied or air. The voice is the *cantus firmus* of every music, underlying form, instrumentation, harmony and style. It is the one universal tone that transcends place and time. The man who cannot carry a tune is an exception. Vocal melody is as natural as speech, and is acquired unconsciously at the same early stage. When we speak of music as a universal language, it is *singing* we mean, not its particular instrumental and harmonic offshoots, which are seldom translatable across the barriers of remote cultures and races. The Japanese ceremonial music is not in our grain, nor would a Brahms symphony convey much to the Watusi of the African Equatorial Plateau. But we have a real kinshp with the *folk song* of these lands, and they with ours. In their song we can feel sorrow and gaiety, energy and lassitude, love and hate. We could easily learn their songs, and they ours, while an instrumental interchange is quite another thing. We have in common the organs of breathing and speech; and our bodily rhythms, our walking, swinging of the arms, and heartbeat are alike.

Indeed, when we strip music of its cultured clothes, we find,

32

as in painting, that the human body is its first model. But instead of *seeing* its contours and postures, we *feel* the body's movements, and its rhythms; our sentences and phrases correspond to the breath. We feel the sensations of strain and release, pain and pleasure: systole and diastole. What we hear substantiates what we feel. *The physiological man is music's primary source.* And his speech is the prosaic model of his melody.

It is true that sounds of nature (the pulse of waves, the sighing of trees, the melody of birds) all these are also models; but it is because of their human aspects and parallels that they have become so. It is those sounds in nature that have pulse, rhythm and tone that we call musical.[1]

We cannot assume, then, as Schopenhauer and many others have, that music is by nature an abstract art, differing thus from poetry and painting. It differs only in that its model is not apparent to the eye or the ear. We are obliged to turn within rather than look or listen without. But the distinction remains nebulous. Will anyone say that Rembrandt or Michelangelo looked only without? Instead, the greatest of paintings have the quality of inwardness, in the same measure as the greatest of symphonies. Likewise a man of letters reads into his subjects what he has discovered in exploring himself; though it is also true that he learns to know himself through the study of others. Outwardness and inwardness are mutual and interdependent, and we can use the terms only against each other. Nothing is more misleading than the absolute concept of subjectivity and objectivity. It is no idle paradox of Samuel Butler's when he says that a portrait portrays the painter rather than his subject. Failing a proper distinction here, modern art (notably painting declaring non-

---

[1] As in painting, El Greco's Toledo sky, Turner's sea, or Van Gogh's flame-like cypresses, so Beethoven's *Kreutzer Sonata*, Chopin's *A Minor Etude*, or Moussorgsky's *Bald Mountain*, are exciting largely because of their wild human gesture. *The artist humanizes nature; but does not imitate it.* The *Pastorale Symphony* is man in a benevolent countryside. In contrast, there is what Tovey calls, "the expensive realism of the dozen muted brass instruments which in Strauss' *Don Quixote* accomplish in ten rehearsals what a flock of sheep achieve extempore"— which, however, deserves to be construed as a piece of bravura rather than a mere dull imitation.

objectivity its aim), and the older art (say, of David in France which strives for verisimilitude), are beating around the same bush, only from opposite sides. In both, objectivity assumes an undue importance, either by denial or emphasis. The result is a materialist art.

The painter's cult of nonobjectivity has today invaded music. It takes on a variety of forms, most all of which entail some kind of *avoidance* (avoidance of the accepted grammar: the common cadences, common meters, sequences, tonalities), but its principal outward manifestation is an unadulterated instrumentalism that has broken all ties with the voice. The child has renounced his ancestor, for were not all string and wind instruments conceived of originally to imitate, support, and decorate the human voice? Now the clarinet, the piano, the violin, the trumpet, and the saxophone, with any one of which nearly anything is possible, become the models for the voice to imitate, instead of the reverse. Essentially this is what Mahler meant, in the remark: "We of today all proceed from the piano, whereas the old masters stem from the violin and the voice." It accounts for the *demelodization* of modern music. But its votaries will not admit this. Instead, they profess an intimate bond with the age of Palestrina (purest affectation, of course). In America where opera has never yet taken a firm hold, and where the song, as a recognized field of "serious" composition, is almost absent,[2] instrumentalism has achieved its apogee. Various writers of music here have entirely by-passed the human voice in their early, more formative writings, coming back to it later, if at all, with a vocalism that is not vocal, and a melodic declamation that embraces its model no more tenderly than the Iron Virgin of Nuremberg. In our schools we have advanced the band to the front rank of musical activity, rather than the chorus. Even instrumental chamber music is no longer a stepchild.

The solo recital singer has nearly disappeared, being accepted, and then rarely, only by virtue of his operatic, or television, fame.

---

[2] We find it necessary to borrow the German word *lied* in order to distinguish from the popular, folk, or "entertainment" song.

There are graduate students in our colleges who will dissect a fugue, a passacaglia or a sonata at the drop of a hat, who will machine-gun you with historical dates, names and doctrines; yet for whom the Schubert songs are but an episode to be listed with some indulgence in the grand "evolutionary" flight from a past that never was to a future no one would wish to experience. Mention the songs of Beethoven, Schumann, and Brahms, of Liszt, Moussorgsky, and Debussy, and an evasive hint of recollection is the best you can hope for.

Altogether, the singer is in a bad way today. He has virtually no profession to turn to, after his schooling. Instead of the fifty or so opera houses of Western Germany, or the forty-odd in Italy, and Soviet Russia, America has only two or three repertory houses. The operas like San Francisco or St. Louis, splendid as their productions are, are as yet little more than temporary tent-platforms, so long as they supply a local orchestra and chorus only, and do not harbor under their roof a staff of their own conductors, stage directors, and principal singers. Even the oratorio, with its adjunct of professional soloists, is underdeveloped here by comparison with England and Canada. Witness that Bach and Handel, the crowning figures of the oratorio, are known virtually by no more than one or two choral works each. Here a singer can survive, apart from the vulgar and ubiquitous world of advertising, only by teaching.

In the academic world, singing is damaged by an undue emphasis on theoretical and musicological studies that look with condescension upon the most instinctive and natural of musical expressions, and foist upon it demands of "learning" that are not only inappropriate, time-consuming and wasteful, but are often actually injurious. "Musicianship" is set up as a singer's goal, rather than artistry; and knowledge triumphs over beauty, of which it should be but an adjunct. Even the matter of language is misunderstood in our colleges, where we impose years of formal study in foreign tongues, at the cost of serious studies in the repertory, when everyone ought to know that a foreign language is only properly learned in its native land. It can, how-

ever, be picked up as to sound by anyone with a sensitive ear,
given the right model and perhaps a little phonetical aid. Meanwhile we neglect our own excellent language, decrying it as unmusical, because it has not the "pure" vowels of the Italian, and
seldom study its own particular vocal idiosyncracies. At the
same time we overlook the most perfect models of the musical
use of English: namely the Elizabethan songs of Dowland, Campion, Rosseter; or the madrigals of Weelkes, Wilbye, and Byrd;
not to forget the songs and operas of the later Purcell. The tiresome debate about opera in English goes on after generations,
fostered, I am bound to admit, not by Europeans, but by ourselves. We must have the opera pure, as if the public were not
entitled to know what is happening on the stage, and as if the
language of Shakespeare, Milton, and Whitman were not good
enough for music.

Dvorak remarked: "If the Americans had a chance to hear
grand opera sung in their own language, they would enjoy it
as well and appreciate it as highly as the opera-goers of Vienna,
Paris or Munich enjoy theirs. The change from Italian and
French to English may have the effect of improving the voices
of the American singers, bringing out more clearly the beauty
and strength of the timbre, while giving an intelligent conception
of the words that enables singers to use pure diction, which
cannot be obtained in a foreign tongue." Granting the superiority
of any opera properly sung in the language it was conceived in,
my own experience includes hearing the worst performance of
Carmen ever, at the Comique in Paris in French, and the best
ever at the Staatsoper in Vienna, in German. I remember also
hearing the *Barber of Seville* at Central City, Colorado, so pre-
sented as to make me totally unaware that Rossini had not
written the work in English. Words and music went together
as deftly as in Gilbert and Sullivan.

What we need is good and lively translations; and this requires poets, not grammarians. We need to study the musical
declamation of our English poetry. We need conductors, coaches,
and stage directors who understand the genius of our native

tongue; and who do not superimpose on English singing the idiosyncracies of another language. The musical heart of most opera, apart from Wagner where it lies in the orchestra, is found in the arias and concerted numbers. In these the demands of melody so formalize the words, extending, repeating, and embellishing them, that nearly any language can supplant the original without musical loss. It is in the recitatives and all the more nearly speech-like portions that we must make musical concessions to whatever language is being used. But since in recitative the music is usually of secondary importance, this too can be done without artistic loss. Better clear words than "correct" note-values, wherever the melody happens to be of secondary import. It is time our operas Americanize themselves to the degree that the Staatsoper in Vienna has become Austrian, the Paris Opera, French, and Covent Garden, English.

Composers, too, have a need to be understood in the light of their native culture and history, rather than by a technical comparison with their contemporaries abroad, who have a different dish to prepare—perhaps as yet a subtler one. Not until such conditions have been remedied may we expect great native opera, nor indeed, a proportionate share of great singers, to come forth. *They need a home in order to be at home.* Verdi did not write for the Maryinski Theatre of Russia, nor Sir Arthur Sullivan for the Dresden Opera House, nor Strauss for La Scala. The answer is as simple as that.

It is quite possible that some of the best musical writing in America has taken the modest form of song. We are already one of the richest countries in folk song—a literature which stems from backgrounds as numerous and diverse as our melting pot, but more particularly from the land of our principal language. Our folk song has been described by John Powell as being *older* than most of Western Europe's because of the two-century-long isolation of Appalachia during the modernization of all Western Europe.

Our first successful efforts in composition are found to be in the hymns, revival songs, and white spirituals. There then followed figures like Stephen Foster, whose songs are known throughout the world and are quite properly looked on now as American folk song. George F. Root and Henry Clay Work are the authors of some of the greatest marching songs in history, those of the Civil War. MacDowell, the first of our major instrumental writers, left a considerable body of songs, not his best works by any means, but worthy nevertheless. Griffes surpassed him in this field; and about this time came Charles Ives, surely the most experimental, independent, and prolific composer of songs of his day—an American Gesualdo, if not a Moussorgsky. Ives, one of the most successful insurance men in the business, published a book of songs and gave them away gratis to anyone who would have them, assuring thereby, if not intentionally, their prompt and utter neglect in a country that values its products by their sales. Since his death, we are beginning to know these songs; and we might well be led to infer from the experience of a man wealthy enough to publish privately, but honorable enough not to buy favor and fame, that there may be treasures of song by other native composers waiting similarly for the blessings of posthumous recognition.

The eras of song writing have usually accompanied or followed eras of lyric poetry. Dowland, Campion, and Rosseter were contemporary with Shakespeare; the lives of Schubert and Schumann overlapped those of Goethe and Heine; more recently, Warlock and Williams have been roughly contemporary with Housman and Yeats.

In America we have a wealth of lyric poetry calling for song, particularly the contributions of the women, beginning with Emily Dickinson and succeeded by Edna Millay, Sara Teasdale, Elinor Wiley, and Marianne Moore. Frost, Sandburg, and Jeffers are not primarily lyricists in the accepted musical sense; likewise, Cummings, Eliot, and Williams. But who will say what is poetry needing song?

Some poetry is too close to being music itself to call for more, for instance, Poe. Some poetry is unmusical, or at least not evocative of music (I shall not lay myself open to literary

derision by naming any poet). Some poems are too long to
handle, and some are too purely intellectual or epigrammatic,
as for example, Pope. But tastes vary, and no one has yet
discovered the infallible mark of a poem's fitness for music,
unless it be the composer's special genius, to which nearly all
materials will bend.

Words and music have combined to form a significant recent
song literature, of which all too little is yet known; for example:
E. E. Cummings with Paul Nordoff; Gertrude Stein with Virgil
Thomson; Walter de la Mare with Theodore Chanler; Tennessee
Williams, with both Ned Rorem and Paul Bowles; John Clare
and Rilke with David Diamond; Tagore with John Alden Carpenter; Matthew Arnold with Samuel Barber; Yeats with John Ed-
munds; Thoreau, Longfellow, and Whittier with Charles Ives.
This is but a mere sketch of what exists; so much, as yet, remains
unknown, unpublished, and unrecorded.

While the poem usually precedes the song, it sometimes
happens the other way about. Burns wrote many of his lyrics to
existing melodies. Some poets wrote with certain—often the
same—tunes floating about in the background. I have heard
it said Yeats was one of these. "Having a chune," he called it.
Thomas Campion was both poet and composer. Melody and
accompaniment may each lead in the inspiration of the other.
The songs of Mozart and Beethoven certainly grew mostly out
of the vocal line; it is quite possible, however, that many of the
songs of Hugo Wolf grew out of the piano part. The two alter-
natives, nevertheless, do not obviate simultaneity of conception,
surely the commonest process. The difference is perhaps one
of emphasis.

As to what activates musical thought in song, there is little
agreement between writers. A particular feeling is doubtless
at the root. It may even happen that a musical motif, be that
harmony, melody, figuration, or rhythm, will go in search of
appropriate words. Or again, the composer may be obsessed
with the timbre of a certain voice, and then fashion his music,
or seek out words, for it. "If you ask me," said Mendelssohn,

"what I was thinking of when I wrote it, I would say: just the song as it stands. . . . The thoughts which are expressed to me by music that I love are not too indefinite to be put into words, but on the contrary, too definite." Composing involves a kind of prescience in the grace of which nearly any combination appears manageable, producing at the time an agony of riches, along with just enough memory of the day-to-day poverty of ideas, as to cause wonder why this delicious state cannot be evoked at will at any time. Needless to say, it is a flowering of thought that presupposes an extensive and arduous cultivation of habits; and in that way is quite analogous to performance and the long study and practice that go before it.

We often distinguish strophic songs from those that are "through-composed" (a wretched translation of the German *durch-komponiert,* another term deserving extinction). Wagner and Moussorgsky are admired for the way they fit music to all of a poem's declamatory contours. The "classical" composers and Schubert are usually content to capture the prevalent meaning of a poem in one more general design of accompaniment or melody or both, which they will then pursue, preludewise, throughout the song. They leave to the singer the more intimate adjustment to the different vagaries of the text. As to the merits of these approaches, Tovey says, "The strophic song, with the same tune for several stanzas, condemned as lazy and low by our prose critics of music, becomes, as Brahms always maintained, the highest achievement of a songwriter."

This brings us around again to the folk song, which is nearly always of this character, the envy of whoever has tried to write melody. We give the name "art song" to the opposite, as if it were something superior. Nobody has ever enlightened us as to why a folk song is not a work of art just because its author is usually unknown, or because it may have been born out of a group sentiment—as we may assume that some of the spirituals and work songs were. Most of the folk songs stand on their melodic merit alone, seldom needing, though often inviting, accompaniment. Of how many "art songs" could this be said?

What would be *Die Lotusblume* of Schumann without the piano; or songs such as: *Verborgenheit* of Wolf, *Morgen* of Strauss, *Im Treibhaus* of Wagner, any one of the "Sunless" cycle of Moussorgsky, or the *Erlkönig* of Schubert?

The folk song as a basis for composition is common to most periods. The early Lutheran Church borrowed from this very source for its harmonized chorals, many of which were worked into the fabric of Bach's greatest works. Haydn dipped liberally into Croatian folk song. Beethoven, commissioned to make settings of Irish and Scotch songs, "Beethovenized" these, as we would expect and indeed wish. Superb as were Liszt's and Brahms' uses of Hungarian Gypsy lays, it was Bartok in our time who finally explored the true Magyar melodies, incorporating this experience into a unique personal style. The modern Spanish writers, Albeniz and De Falla are unthinkable without that peculiar blend of Spanish, Gypsy and Moorish strains that we now think of as Spanish folk song. The United States, like Russia a century before, remained rather aloof toward its folk songs until about the twenties. Since then it has been devouring and exploiting them at a rate that is almost alarming and may drive their few remaining original exponents either into hiding, or into the arms of the juke box. We can safely predict that the age of our folk song is coming to an end, a victim of communication, highways, and electricity, and all the enemies of isolation, and finally the appetite of commerce and its immodest mistress, advertising.

Folk song in the meantime, however, has inspirited the writings of many of our composers. That tendency is a healthy antidote to the abstractions and the instrumental excesses to which our concert world has been subject for so long.

We come now to the point where we may ask what may be done to stimulate the song. Though not a profitable venture, good recordings are needed. Some patronage and foundational help, as well as the cooperation of singers and teachers, are essential. Even the recorded repertoire of the classics deserves expansion and renewal. Many of the greatest songs—one might say a majority—have never been recorded. How many songs of Dowland, Purcell, Mozart, Beethoven, Liszt, or even Schubert and Brahms, can you procure on records? Always the same few are recorded, while a major literature remains unknown.

Song literature courses of broad coverage should be in all college curricula. Can it be said that the fugues of Bach are really more "basic" than the songs of Schubert? Though I am not a great believer in prizes, I nevertheless would like to see inducements held out for songs, comparable to those offered for symphonies. Has anyone ever heard of a commission or prize for a song cycle?

Nevertheless, we need not believe that anything fundamental is accomplished with prizes.[3] "Such stimulants," said Charles Ives, "tend to industrialize art rather than develop its spiritual sturdiness. . . . A cocktail will make a man eat more, but will not give him a healthy normal appetite."

[3] Today we have a veritable plethora of prizes. The public has little doubt that musical awards are as clear-cut as those in athletics. It forgets that while in the latter a quantitative measurement is usually possible (the time, the score, the height, the distance), in the former the competition is one of qualities which cannot be compared on a measurable basis. At the same time that competition in performance may have some merit, competition in composing is meaningless. The bringing to life of any score, let alone a complex score for orchestra, is an arduous process to which few judges have the time, patience, and insight to lend themselves. If a conductor of the caliber of Gabrilowitsch preferred not to pass judgment on new orchestral scores until he had read them through with his Detroit Orchestra (why have such readings not continued?), who then are the judges who can estimate a work's worth on a mere "dry" reading? There are a small few who can formulate the sounds, but that is not the same as capturing the spirit, which invokes the body as well as the mind.

Once a prize has been awarded, it is easy for the conductor, the society, or the club to relieve itself of further responsibility toward the composers, the best of whom may have learned from experience to have too little confidence in contests to warrant the trouble and expense of competing again.

I am not a little embarrassed at all the competitions that now limit candidacy to *Americans alone.* This has a discriminatory, inhospitable flavor, and could be construed as evidence that we fear the competition of those from abroad. Apart from the aspersion on native talent, I am not impressed with such an obvious gesture of nationalism while at the same time Americans are prevented from competing openly for positions of real responsibility. *The proper food for artistic growth is usefulness and activity in society.* Since music is a multibillion-dollar business in our land, there should be room for our qualified professionals in every branch of the art.

Of all music, singing touches most nearly on the national problem, since it involves the use of our language. We need not be surprised, therefore to find it the most neglected of our musical offspring. If there are to be reforms in our music, let us begin with singing.

THE CRITIC

He pays too high a price
    For knowledge and for fame
Who sells his sinews to be wise,
    His teeth and bones to buy a name
And crawls through life a paralytic
    To earn the praise of bard and critic.

RALPH WALDO EMERSON

Criticism requires James Whitcomb Riley to sing no more till he can sing like Shakespeare.
MARK TWAIN

Limits of Criticism

"A man may utter with impunity that which he cannot publish with impunity," said Fenimore Cooper. "The distinction arises from the greater circulation and the greater power to injure, of a published libel than of a spoken slander." There are two realms that are fairly immune from the ordinary libel restrictions, politics and the arts. The probable reason is that both thrive on publicity. They go on the theory that anything that is said about a politician or an artist is better than nothing said at all. It is more important in politics and art that the public know a man's name than to know what he stands for. A well-advertised scoundrel may well have more of a following than an obscure saint.

"The worst thing you can do to an author," said Dr. Johnson, "is to be silent as to his works. An assault upon a town is a bad thing, but starving it is still worse." Thus, musicians, while they may resent censure in print, and express themselves frequently as wishing to see all criticism stopped, would pause before eliminating the present practice. They need, above all, to be known.

The reputation of a surgeon gets around by word of mouth, through his patients, his colleagues and students, and through the hospitals. The clientele this brings him is sufficient to occupy his time and energies, and to provide an income. The music teacher, at the turn of the century, enjoyed a similar degree of independence. Men like MacDowell, Foote, Chadwick, Ziehn, Joseffy, Gunn, in fact, the greater number of superior artists not engaged in conducting and concertizing, taught privately, achieved independence, and made a good and respected living at it. If they joined forces with a college or conservatory, it was from choice rather than necessity. Today nearly all music is institutionalized. Only those who teach children can afford to be independent. A degree from a college, or university, or even from a conservatory—for conservatories have added the trappings of academic life—will do more for a student's career than a certificate of study with the greatest of living artists; and the students, influenced by the prevalent trend, frankly say they are more interested in this kind of "security" than in mastery.

But the touring virtuoso, the conductor, and the composer who aspires to performance and publication, must advertise himself. Word-of-mouth opinion has lost all importance outside the little village of New York's musical headquarters. Opinion is like the human voice in the face of modern electronics, whereby a whimper can be magnified into a continental roar while the lustiest tones unaided go as unheard as the single voice challenging a hurricane at the seashore. So the artist purchases space in musical magazines or elsewhere, which is expensive. Obviously then, if he receives editorial attention in the metropolitan newspapers, the musician must consider himself fortunate, whatever its tone.

The music editors, or critics, know all this; and it happens seldom that they belabor a man in the public eye to the point of creating an unfavorable balance, even when his equipment as a musician is questionable. Besides, the borderlines of professionalism in art are vague. The doctor's degree in medicine, while it does not establish a man's talent, does at least certify his educational background, and is therefore something of a key to his learning. The doctorate in music tells nothing as to the person's capacity as an artist; and certifies only that he has spent a vast amount of time in libraries and classrooms, which are by no means the same thing as laboratories and clinics in the sciences. Numerous great artists have taught themselves, or at least have received no formal education. But there are no recognized doctors who did not go to medical school. And then, our very lives depend on medical skill. Who can say that life cannot go on without music? No one was ever known to *unlearn* anatomy in an anatomical laboratory, but the number of those who have unlearned singing in voice studios, or dissipated their talents in libraries, is impressive. Scientific knowledge has never hurt a doctor. But an excess of factual and theoretical knowledge of music has injured, warped, constipated, and undone many a good talent. "A man's ignorance," said Thoreau, speaking obviously not of doctors, "is something not only useful but beautiful, while his knowledge, so called, is oftentimes worse than useless, besides being ugly." There is no visible, exact, or definable fence in music separating right from wrong, good from bad, beautiful from ugly, or true from false. But for the doctor's patient there is the indisputable line of demarcation between survival and death.

Where, then, is the threshold of libel in criticism?

The important consideration in publishing an official opinion, is to make clear that this is only the critic's opinion, and not fact. You may say of a composer that a given piece is boresome, or even badly constructed; but you cannot decently say he does not know how to write music, for this is professional slander. You can assault the work, but not the man; otherwise you abuse the prerogative of your office. You are there *to express personal taste rather than pass judgment*. In the journal of Alice James, sister of Henry and William, we read, "It is reassuring to hear the English pronouncement that Emily Dickinson is fifth-rate." Benjamin Franklin remarked, "I wish all well-meaning, sensible men would not lessen their power of doing good by a positive and assuming manner that seldom fails to disgust, tends to create opposition, and to defeat every one of those purposes for which speech was given us."

The very man whose knowledge and experience give his judgments value, might well be the most reluctant to make them, were he in a position to do so. For he knows that it is easier to blame than it is to praise, that acknowledgment of the accomplishment of another implies a degree of self-criticism, where denunciation is often only self-praise. He is in the advantageous position of bully, for his adversary remains weaponless. "He can smite," says H. L. Mencken, "without being smitten. He challenges other men's work, and is exposed to no comparable challenge of his own. The more reputations he breaks, the more his own reputation is secured."

He would have difficulty deciding between being essentially an appraiser of values and an entertainer of his reading public, knowing that the majority of readers prefers entertainment at the cost of truth, to truth at the cost of entertainment. Hanslick entertained his Viennese readers for years with his Wagnerian libels. What remains today is Wagner's characterization of Hanslick in the character of Beckmesser; and, of course, Wagner's great music.

The conscientious critic recognizes within himself a conflict between the claims of literature and those of music. If he abandons himself to hearing a great performance, he is apt to be left with little to say about it. Abject or unqualified adoration offers little of literary interest. Or, should he permit himself to formulate a fine literary statement during the progress of a concert, can he at the same time absorb the music to the full? For, as La Bruyère said, "The pleasure of criticism deprives us of that of being moved by beautiful things."

The critic is also aware that there may be depths in a work, and even in a performance that cannot be comprehended on the first hearing; and he would know, too, that a work may possess legitimate charms, which are nevertheless incapable of weathering the exploitative repetition which any successful work will undergo. In other words, is he to give us first or final impressions?

He realizes that it is quite impossible to know what is in a new work when it is misread by the interpreter; and that it is also seldom possible to know if the fault lies in the work or in its reading. A mediocre work finely performed will succeed where a fine work badly read will fail. He would remember that some of the greatest masterpieces suffered partial or complete failure through some such causes; and that other great masterpieces never came to light in their author's time at all. (Pursuing this same train of thought, he might reason that there are likely to be masterpieces which never will be uncovered.)

He remembers also that a great to-do was made over writers and works which proved of no consequence a generation or two later; and that it is not unlikely that many of the big-wigs of today will collapse no less, on reappraisal by coming generations.

The thoughtful appraiser learns, from these misjudgments of the past, to consider the judgments of the present to be no less vulnerable (including his own). He might even allow that some of the opinions of the past, which were later reversed, had substance for their time; that is to say that even posterity is not the only infallible judge.

He may reflect that possibly music should be judged on many different levels: music for youth, for middle age, for old age; music for one hearing, for two hearings, for indefinite hearings; music for full concentration, for part concentration, for no concentration at all. It may occur to him that perhaps the fixed yardstick of permanent value, profundity, or perfection, is manifestly improper and, if applied conscientiously, leads to all sorts of absurd compromises when confronted with the transient and varied aspects and needs of music-making.

He knows that with American centralization has come an ever increasing reputational maldistribution, a fact no less pernicious than the fact of immense wealth battening on dire poverty, and that it should be his aim to be more critical with the famous than with the obscure, instead of the prevalent contrary. What good is it to add yet another voice to those vast choruses of praise that cannot contribute a mite to the stature of an already celebrated personage, and that often embarrass him, as well as the reader, with their excess? He is aware, too, that too much praise often leads to a resentful reaction.

He must consider that America, being at once a vast heterogeneous country and a highly centralized one, could scarcely be known by what transpires in two or three auditoriums in New York City. Yet it takes at the same time its musical cue almost entirely from a half dozen newspapers and magazines, one or two management offices, one union office, three or four radio stations, and a few recording studios, all in Manhattan. Consequently, the appraisal of a new work or personality in the metropolitan press imposes on him a responsibility out of all proportion to the occasion.

In short, realizing his own power, and the vaster powers bestowed upon a few other persons with whom he rubs shoulders nearly every day, in this musical bottleneck, the critic should be working toward the abrogation of such power. He should do this in direct violation of self-interest, toward a better distribution of the fruits, no less than the labors, of culture throughout the land, in the more general interests of music. He should become, and indeed he sometimes is, a champion of decentralization.

If he has any modesty, if he realizes that criticism is not the reason for music but only an appendage to it, if he respects all real musical competence, particularly when it is greater than his own, if he gives thought to all these and corollary considerations, the good critic is apt to feel it is best to say nothing at all. But this very realization is what most entitles him to pass opinions on to a public that feels it must and will have them.

So then, what should he do?

The rule is simple. *He should write on his own level.* If he is a trained professional, then he can be expected to pass professional opinions within the framework, not of the journalistic, but the musical, amenities. If he is an amateur, he has an equal right to speak his reactions, provided they are not passed off as professional opinions. If he is a scholar, there is no call for him to pretend to more perhaps than historical interest in the high G's of tenors, or the record speed of a pianist's *Islamey*. Let him be honest. Honesty means also that he may not pretend to an authority he has not. A little ignorance is a dangerous thing. Nevertheless, it is better to be half-learned and enthusiastic rather than learned and weary.

If he does not care for music, he has no right whatever to his post. But prejudices he may and should have. The "dispassionate" critic is no critic at all. A man without feelings, and strong feelings at that, has no right to speak publicly about an art that is all feeling. "It is the capacity for making good or bad art a personal matter that makes a man a critic," says Shaw. "The artist who accounts for my disparagement by alleging personal animosity on my part is quite right: when people do less than their best, and do that less at once badly and self-complacently, I hate them, loathe them, detest them. . . . In the same way, really fine artists inspire me with the warmest personal regard. . . ."

On Musical Stature

Watching the general drift of today's music, the art seems to "recede on one side as fast as it gains on the other." In Emerson's words: "It acquires new arts and loses old instincts." Its apparent progress is later seen to have been only change. The new always imagines it surpasses the old, but in time we see that it has mainly supplanted it. Youth's bond with the future, and age's bond with the past together make the cycle of generations. Systems and schools rise, are emulated for a brief space, and then disappear, leaving only the most characteristic landmarks, often ruins, of great thought. Forever the erosion of time. The vast masses of others' work that underlay these crowning achievements are soon forgotten. We single out one master and then compress the course of his entire life work into a few hours of concentrated inspiration, disregarding the endless stretches of preparation, imitation, uncertainty, ennui, trial and error, failure, procrastination, distraction, and frustration that lay between these peaks of his achievement. We *symphonize* a great life, discarding all but what is essential for a well-proportioned biographical picture.

We hear of the man who "freed" music. It has a brave sound, but then we presently ask: what tyranny did he free us of? I

54

am sure Beethoven never presumed to imagine he "freed" us of Mozart. Did Mozart perhaps "free" us of Bach? Or did Haydn give us the sonata? I think he did better than that. He gave us some very fine music. If Beethoven, or Wagner, or Monteverde "freed" music it was for themselves alone they did it, and the freeing was not from their predecessors, but from what a subsequent generation had made out of these. As in religion, a great artist has invariably disciples who begin to make of their master a new tyrant.

The past is as a mountain range in the distance. Its mass and silhouette are clear, and its main peaks stand out unmistakably. Of its foothills, moraines, forests, and streams; of its intimate topography; of its valleys reaching upward with treelike divarication, we have only a vague conception borne out of our own time and experience.

Perhaps we are on another range ourselves, not yet standing at its summit; and so our glance takes in, not its own topmost summits, but only the trees or the nearby canyon walls. We have, of course, no map. Good maps of any age are made only from afar. We are uncertain of our destination and have little knowledge of anything beyond our immediate surroundings. For a while we grope upward through the dense underbrush. At length we pass the timber line, and the vista becomes more broad. Viewing the past range from a distance and the present range at close quarters, we possess no instrument of mutual estimate; there is no common focus. Quite properly, then, we abandon the absolute estimate in favor of the relative. Emerson's *Monadnock* is not even a foothill in the Himalayas, but it is an Everest in southern New Hampshire. There is no need to translate the New Hampshire summit into Tibet and rob it of local dignity.

We happen to live in an age just removed from one of the greatest musical ranges in history. It is a temptation to say of a living man, particularly when he aspires to great things, "He is no Beethoven," which says no more than that he lives under a great shadow. But the valleys surrounding the Matterhorn are well watered and the grass is still green. One may well say, without loss of reverence for genius, that Beethoven is not there to oppress, but to be emulated. He teaches us to live and not to grovel.

We recollect the Matterhorn and wonder. What meets the eye today is something leveling, a pull away from the mountains, a fear of their grandeur and dignity. Someone asked Debussy if he loved the Alps. "Ah, no," he said, "they are too high." The principal new landmarks begin to be a dreary proletarianism, a cocksure sort of learning, a sour sentimentality which nourishes itself on the denial of sentiment, and a self-generated, didactic fury.

Composers easily tend to become suspicious of dignity. If they are by nature tall, they affect a stoop to conceal their stature. Dignity is looked on as a pose, or the mark of a deposed aristocracy. The gentleman is suspect. In oafishness we read honesty, in manners hypocrisy. Observe in the movies and television that it is usually the villains who are courteous; and the heroes are mostly honest louts, the taming of whose boorishness by the heroine constitutes the high point of sentimental drama.

But the hunger for the mountains remains. You breathe good air when you hear *The Messiah*. The public unwittingly responds to grander art. It senses the compliment to humanity in a noble musical statement. As the gentleman invites the gentleman in you, so does dignity call forth the dignity of the beholder. *It allows him to realize his own stature.*

Now comes along this matter of talent. They say of an artist, "He succeeded in doing what he set out to do." They praise him for that, overlooking what the aim was: extolling the success at the cost of the motive. Or again, they dwell on the sense of hearing for itself. "How well scored," is a familiar tribute among musicians, or, "It sounds so well." And then again, how ready they are to unburden the artist of all social responsibility. "What has the art to do with the man?" "I am not interested in his politics or his morals. I care only about his art."

"Is your music then merely a tinkle?" asked Confucius. Are

we concerned only with an exercise? Has music no principles, no ethics; has humanity no part in it? Is it enough to know how well sounds are tailored for the ear? Shall the ancient themes be sealed off because we have invented a new toy for the senses or the brain? What about life and death, youth and age, love and hate, peace and war, humor and sorrow? What about tenderness, exaltation, resignation. What about worship? Have our new devices rendered them obsolete?

"Ah, but he is so clever; . . . so very consistent; . . . so logical; . . . so ingenious; . . . so experimental; . . . such a wonderful contrapuntalist; . . . his form is so unimpeachable." All very well. These virtues abound in all the great masters, but we take them for granted. If a man is an athlete, do we speak of his superb digestion, circulation, or metabolism? Any master of the past would have blushed to be praised as the promulgator of some special theory or technique. "I am distressed," said Monet, "at having been the cause of the name given to a group." (The Impressionists.)

Has anyone ever heard of a Bach or a Beethoven theory, or a Chopin "technique," or a Brahms "method"? Indeed these men were the most methodical of all; their craft was inventive beyond all formula: "technically quite easy to describe," as Thomas Mann puts it, "and yet quite indescribable." In theory, their resourcefulness could not be encompassed in a dozen books, since every work was a new experiment. "It is time to say farewell," said Busoni, "to the subdividing of music based on its forms, and on the means it employs . . . the sole differences consist in contents and quality."

And how are we to separate a man from his work? If Wagner was at times arrogant, so is his music arrogant. If he was long-winded so are his scores often long-winded. If he was pompous, so was his music pompous. But the noble passages in his music convince me also of the nobility in the man. The endearing musical passages convince me of his endearing personal qualities. The generosity of a Hans Sachs reveals a generosity in Wagner no less. How will you account for the devoted personal following that included Bülow, Klindworth, D'Albert, Cornelius, Richter, King Ludwig, Baudelaire, and Liszt?

We are ever driven back to the realization that a man's art is himself, and that if it is not, it is inferior. The better the art is, the closer does it come to being the man. Every artist worthy of the name makes it his constant business to strive for a truthful statement of himself. Every pretense away from this reveals itself soon enough. For in a sense the artists who succeed one another are all the most diligent detectives, tirelessly seeking out the truth and falsehood of all past utterances, rejecting and accepting without cease. It is part of the process whereby taste is cultivated, wherein a man discovers his affinities. The artist gets to know the personality more intimately than even a psychiatrist. In the end, if the man himself was not great, we abandon his work to oblivion.

Moreover, it makes little difference whether an author—literary, musical or otherwise—speaks of, or imagines, himself as his subject matter or not. He *is* the subject, even though he writes a story about others, or uses another's musical theme, or paints the portrait of another—all, of course, with varying emphasis. I am often struck with a remark such as: "Goethe's work was essentially autobiographical." Well, whose wasn't?

Thus was Moussorgsky a greater figure in music than Debussy, who was much the more educated and subtle artist. Of Debussy, Jean de Reszke once said, "Yes, yes, but that music is for bored people; and I am not bored." Could anyone say this about *Boris Godunov?* Beethoven and Wagner are both immeasurable giants in music, yet Beethoven ennobles his hearer, while Wagner, incomparable painter and magician though he is, tends to depress him. Beethoven's genius liberates; Wagner's enslaves—possibly because of his overweening erotic sensuality, in the expression of which he became the supreme master of all time. Whoever has learned from Beethoven, whether it be Schubert, Brahms, Tschaikovsky, Berlioz, Mendelssohn, Verdi, or even Wagner himself, has acquired something of his forthright, heroic bent. Those who have learned from Wagner have inevitably been strangely devitalized, and sapped of clear vigor and masculine integrity.

"I breathe with difficulty," said Nietzsche, "as soon as Wagner's music begins to act on me." Or Hugo Wolf: "After the intoxicating narcosis of Wagner's art, Beethoven's music seems like heavenly ether and woodland breezes. The former takes my breath away and dashes me to the ground, but the latter expands the lungs and frees the spirit, and veritably makes one a good man, just as Wagner's art in its excess degrades one into a worm."

There is something about Wagner that says, "I have done the final thing. There is no further Olympus." There is nothing of this appropriative finality in Beethoven, though his work possesses an inevitability that is well-nigh unmatched. Beethoven's late work revealed that he was in no wise content to rest on the supreme achievements of his middle period, that he knew there were new ranges to be crossed, which he courageously set out to seek. The element of genius was in the highest degree manifest in Wagner. But of Beethoven one could also say, in the words of Albert Schweitzer, here was "a man whose deed was in tune with his character."

Art hath an enemy called ignorance.

BEN JONSON

Criticism in the Provinces

A generation and a half ago a Chicago newspaper decided that music criticism, in order to become more popular, should discard its cultured tone and resort to the vernacular. Since nearly everybody reads the sporting page, it was decided that here would be a good source to find a popular writer. So a sports editor was assigned to cover musical events.

The results were rather unexpected. At first, everybody read his articles. His ignorance was picturesque, his boners were quotable. But having been a conscientious and well-informed writer on football, he could not long stomach his new role as a musical clown; and busied himself to learn what he could about music from books and from friends in the profession. He manfully set out to acquire in months what usually takes years. In the course of time, his articles gained a measure of correctness and conventionality. But now they had lost both the raciness which had endeared him to football fans, and the charm of ignorance which had furnished the musical world a fertile field for ridicule. Fewer and fewer people read them, and at last the newspaper came to realize that its music page had become even duller than before the experiment. Plainly, the whole thing was a failure, and for no other reason than that a sports writer believed that a Beethoven symphony deserved at least as good a report as a football game.

How far this example may have influenced other papers is hard to say. But pretty soon there appeared a whole new crop of provincial music critics; only this time they were gleaned from the politer strata of the society page. Music, at least as far as newspaper publishers were concerned, was high society; wealth clamored for the prestige that goes with conspicuous patronage. The brief space normally allotted to music could easily be filled with an account of a concert's attendance, of notables present, of the prima donna's gown, of the number of encores, of a conductor's graceful left hand. A pianist's technique (meaning his manual athleticism), or a violinist's hauteur, could be enlarged upon without risk; likewise, the miracles of memory needed to direct a symphony without the score, or any variety of factual trivia.

In the course of time, a certain code of noncommitment developed in these critical circles. The reporter was under no circumstances to express an opinion on any musical matter beyond what the public reaction made clear. Now and then there were deviations from this safe role of propriety, and a critic would indulge himself in encomiums that proved no less absurd than his censures. All this troubled the paper's management not the least bit, for to them music was a matter of minor importance. Never were there any objections whatever from readers. Newspapermen being in the business of selling, stretching, and embellishing news, cannot be expected to subscribe to the old Chinese dictum that "those who know are silent, while those who talk are ignorant."

Let us turn the tables and imagine that a society editor were assigned to cover a football game for the pink page. He might deliver himself of something like this: "Yesterday's game proved a brilliant spectacle, replete with glamorous personalities. The old raccoon coat is a rarity today, but the roving eye of ye reporter caught many a lovely mouton, seal, alpaca, and even mink among the colorful afghans of imported Scottish plaid.

The crisp autumnal breezes wafted over players and audience alike, while the fitful sun, peeping through cottony clouds, shimmered glitteringly on the toddling tubas led by the light-stepping, prize-winning, drum majorette. Then our gladiators, looking like space heroes, went into battle. We must confess it was sometimes hard to keep track of the ball, but were relieved to discover that the players had almost the same difficulty. Sometimes it was lost under a vast pile of thrashing arms and legs. Our enjoyment at seeing it thrown deftly through the air now and then was sometimes cut short by the whistle of one of those busy attendants in striped shirts who were always dancing around nervously and carrying on some kind of sema-phore signals. It occurred to us that a very effective device would be to have the entire team push one of its men through the scattered opposition, if indeed it was their object to get the ball ahead. But perhaps we are giving away secrets. The whole spectacle calls for music without a doubt."

It is interesting to speculate on the reception such a review would receive in sporting circles, yet we have enjoyed reviews of this kind on concerts in some good-sized American cities. They deserve a special place in Americana Absurdia. But even indulgence has limits. Today, nearly every larger town has a college, and nearly every college has a department of music, whose humblest instructor is capable of reviewing musical events with a modicum of competence. It would cost a news-paper very little to engage a local academic writer to cover its limited season of musical events. Some of the larger colleges might well consider granting a degree in music criticism. They have the necessary courses to educate the critic: musical theory and history, instrumental and vocal studies, journalism, English composition and literature, foreign languages, general history, musicology, not to speak of philosophy, esthetics, and sociology. Educated criticism would instruct the public, aid the develop-ment of artists, and promote better standards, offering also guidance to some of the patrons and music lovers who cannot always distinguish between the artist and the charlatan, and who more often than not waste their benefactions on ventures and personalities that are the laughingstock of the profession. It would also strengthen the local artistic morale, and help thus in the imperative move toward decentralization. Above all, it would lend a little more dignity to music.

THE AUTHOR

What is this you bring my America?
Is it uniform with my country?

WALT WHITMAN

If you terrify the man of genius with your wretched measured criticism, he will never let himself go, and you will rob him of his naturalness and his enthusiasm.

GIUSEPPE VERDI

The Composer

"It's hard to be a composer today," a young man complained. "There's so little left that hasn't been done before. The musical fields are spent." Like the citizen of the Thirties, the writer is told that his choice is strictly between the *left* and the *right,* with no course in between: on the one hand the tangled path of erudition, on the other the hard-paved road to the popular. He foresees no desirable goal along either. He looks back to olden times when the musical fields were "fresh." What an enviable day, so he imagines, was that of Vivaldi and Purcell, when melody was sparkling and pure; or the day of Monteverde, when chromatic harmonies first tangled ecstatically; or of Haydn, when simplest charm was esteemed. Now, if he writes simply, he will be called puerile, or imitative, or *epigonenhaft* (to use the German), or retrogressive, or at best surrealistic and cynical. He will not be believed. Yet his heart tells him to seek out the gift to be simple.

Whence, he asks, comes this modern interdict on simplicity, this drive into the complex and the recondite? Why may a man not write as he pleases, especially if it pleases his public? Is public acceptance proof of an art's shallowness, as Schönberg believed? Is it not possible to address oneself to the learned

and the unlearned both? And if not, leaving out other considerations, which side is to be trusted? Wagner let Sachs save the
day for music by making his public the judge. It was the public
that sustained Verdi and Tschaikovsky (and of late, Rachmaninoff)
against the indifference and even contumely of the learned.

For the same reason, the categories "serious" and "popular"
are kept separate, despite all the borrowings between them. And
there are purists on each side who persist in prosecuting tres-
passers from the opposite camp. This separation, though now
and then bridged by a Gershwin or a Bernstein, is regrettable,
particularly for the educated artist. I strongly suspect that the
nearest thing to good American opera has been some of the
better movies and certain Broadway musicals. The best serious
talent should be made welcome here, but it seldom is, the conditions being almost insupportable: the ruthless cutting of
scores, the musical ignorance of most theatrical directors, not
to speak of the sheer inaccessibility of the Broadway and Hollywood producers. And now comes television with untold possibilities for opera and ballet, and crying for new, untried marriages
of the eye and ear, yet failing so lamentably in realizing the
responsibilities that accompany public franchise. Doubtless the
tide will someday turn. Perhaps a few more scandals like that
of the quiz programs will do the trick. But we seem to miss the
main point even in these. The scandal was not so much in the
rigging of what is of necessity an entertainment program; rather,
it lay in the debasing of values when an entire nation witnessed
how a few persons, by nightly answering (aided or unaided)
a few questions—the uselessness and incongruity of which was
matched only by the fatty condescension of their statement—
could achieve in minutes a monetary reward equivalent to that
of years of solid industry. How is it with a nation that makes
such cheap currency of its honest labor?

We gamble willingly with everything but artistic genius. We
allow for experiments and mistrials in science and industry, and
think nothing of rocketing billions into the sea. But television,
this great new medium of communication, education, and enter-

tainment, may not be subjected to the hazards of artistic experiment, and we perforce entrust it to hucksters who make of it the chief agency through which, in the words of Robinson Jeffers, "this America settles in the mold of vulgarity, heavily thickening to empire." It is easy to see why the composer today has a difficult choice.

Where will he find the law of his own song? Would a gifted person think along these lines? Indeed, I am sure he often does. The greatest talents are beset with the gravest doubts. And they are not to be put down, whatever the acclaim. "I still remember, round my thirtieth year," said Wagner, "asking myself whether I possessed the capacity to develop an artistic individuality."

"Because my predecessors have already taken as their own all useful and necessary themes, I will do like one who, because of his poverty, is the last to arrive at the fair, and not being able otherwise to provide himself, chooses all the things which others have looked over and not taken, but refused as being of little value. With these despised and rejected wares . . . I will load my modest pack."

What comforting, if sad, words. Well, they are Leonardo da Vinci's. So he, too, felt the need to begin with the leavings.

If a man wishes to fashion something of his own, he may not dwell too long on the achievements of others. "It was my good fortune," said Goethe, "not to encounter Shakespeare until after I had written my *Goetz* and *Egmont*. He might have overwhelmed me and convinced me of my insignificance."

In this scientific day, we hope to find our way out of the dilemma by theory. We examine the arts closely for ingenious new possibilities; but all we get for our pains is pathology. What we fail to do is to look behind the art for whatever it is in life that has always fructified art. Belief seems no more; worship is feeble and confused; faith in man is lost (and is it not this loss of faith in himself that destroys man's faith in God?); there is an expectation of nothingness. In olden times artists created their works to last. They had the comfort of posterity.

Now aspiration toward endurance seems like a flimsy pretence.
Where is posterity today?

Well, the answer is, as always, only tentative. No course is
sure, and none has ever been. The artist never finds the law
of his art until he has already made the art. *The beginning is
not revealed until he has reached the end.* Music and poetry
have no more idea of their destination than had the explorer
who first entered the American wilderness. The pioneer thinks
the journey is worth trying; he has vague premonitions of what
is ahead; and he must be sure he has the energy to persist.
Nothing is more misleading than to try to emulate those who,
in the admired popular phrase, "know exactly what they want."
Few explorations ever ended with the expected result. Columbus
did not set out to discover New York City.

Formerly, composers wrote for the church, or the theatre,
or a patron, or a particular performance or group, or a school, or a
publisher, or a festival. The idea of "absolute" music, a music
self-generated and aiming to be no more than itself, the means
being the end, is of fairly recent origin. It has a touch of what
the Germans call *Schöngeisteln,* which could be vulgarly translated as an esthetic-twittering. It is true, many great works,
sonatas, quartets, and the like were written without external
objective; but if they are good works, they were largely the
product of a momentum generated through service to something
behind music.

Probably the poorest music of our time is the "absolute music"
(sometimes known as "pure" music, i.e., music totally abstracted
from its human sources). It has the additional weakness of pre-
tending to be the best. Despite all the conscientious and well-
intentioned efforts to produce it, the public does not take it to
heart. Every device of harmony, counterpoint and instrumentation is carried to its extreme limits. But oddly enough, nothing
that has been written since the "dissonant" period went into
high gear (with Schönberg, Stravinski, Ives, and Varese) has
come up to the earlier experiments in originality, puissance, and
formal mastery. It is the same here as in painting, where the

early experimenters—Braque, Kandinsky, Klee, Picasso, and Feininger—set a level that their followers can no longer reach. The vitality is not there any more. The impulse toward revolution is long spent, and what remains is only a spurious sort of wildness. "Truth," as Dr. Johnson put it, "is a cow that will yield them no more milk, so they are gone to milk the bull." Of this writing, Ernest Bloch said: "From one tonal exaggeration to another, we have been hurried along until our ears have become actually perverse and incapable of savoring the clean and fresh beauty of old masterpieces. Our appetite increases for still hotter spices, for still wilder complexities." To this utterance, having been made sometime ago, one should add that a new tide has set in, although, in the confusion of the multitude of currents of today, its course is anything but clear. Nevertheless it is a windy and inhospitable environment for the musical author of today to set up his tent in, and the numerical competition is staggering.

Of all those in music, the intellectuals seem to have the greatest staying power. One reads, for example, in a prospectus for Advanced Musical Studies at Princeton University: "The Seminar aims . . . to stress the primacy of musical experience and imagination, insisting on categorical distinctions between artistic production and systematic thought." My, oh my! And now there is the new Electronic Music (Musique Concrète). The "twelve-toners" are still holding many an academic fort; and some of the jazz men are now scaling the ladder of erudition. Yet recent opera has in some instances turned toward simplicity, and there are figures like Karl Orff who create out of the starkest simplicities a kind of medieval surrealism. The wind is changing direction.

Practically speaking, the American composer of today earns little or nothing from his writings. Unlike the literary writer, he has no agencies to promote him in the publishing or performing market (the musical agencies being all for the performing artist), probably because the profits in the former are too small. If he is published, he receives at best ten per cent of gross sales.

Since most publishers remain strangely indifferent to the need
to actively promote their newly printed music, through records,
radio, and reviewing, the sales are invariably small. The only
performances that yield the composer any appreciable revenue
are those over the air; and now and then (ever so seldom) one
by an orchestra in concert. The song writer must consider himself fortunate if he achieves any publication, let alone revenue
therefrom.

If he turns to living poets and dramatists for his texts (which
he ought to do), he is usually taxed by their literary publishers
out of all his profits. In an opera, for example, the labor of the
composer in making merely the piano score, not to speak of the
orchestration, may be ten or fifteen times that of the librettist,
whose agent is likely nevertheless to propose an equal division
of royalties. As for poems, the publishers of these poems exact
fees as if the composer had a market like Irving Berlin's.

As to the press, books are reviewed in every larger newspaper
in the land and in many national magazines, while published
music is reviewed hardly at all, even in the few little trade journals
let alone in our one subsidized scholarly magazine, *The Musical
Quarterly*. A dead silence greets the issuance of musical works
which are, at present rates, very costly to their publishers. Years
ago *The American Mercury* took upon itself the task of reviewing
musical publications, but this worthy effort passed unrewarded,
and I have heard of no similar venture since.

What has happened is that the public has come to approach
its music more and more passively. It knows more about music
today, yet participates in it less. Formerly the amateur learned
the symphonic literature by playing it four-hand on the piano.
Today he learns it from records. This is not to overlook the
growth of active chamber music, and also of amateur and semiprofessional orchestras. But the general picture is one of growing inaction, supplemented with learning at two or three removes
from the source, a state of affairs that receives due encouragement from the colleges. Thus, a musical library today is not
a library of scores, but of records. Few people can now read

music at the piano, and even among teachers there is more and more resort to the convenient phonograph for guidance and incentive. As to recordings of new works, most of the record companies look upon any edition of less than ten to twenty thousand sales as a material loss. Few modern works hold out promise for such a market. Consequently, many of the best new works are not recorded at all. Here again, communication defeats itself, and we are left more ignorant than before.

On those rare instances when a composer's work is played by one of our orchestras, he is likely to be the only person who is not paid at all, unless he has achieved fame or notoriety. He is further taxed to pay the cost of extracting the orchestral parts, averaging around five hundred dollars for a normal length symphony, if he is lucky enough to find a copyist who does not charge by the union scale which would well-nigh double the cost. His status is such that conductors will keep his scores months or perhaps years, sometimes even losing them, without apology or redress. He is reasonably convinced that most scores are not even looked at, for the conductor is withal an overburdened man and new scores are very taxing to read. The usual request on his part to see new scores is mainly a public gesture, well meant perhaps, but usually quite futile; yet costly in time, postage, and self-respect to the writer. "There are so many composers," sighed one conductor, forgetting for the moment the spiraling population of his own calling. "I have not read a new score in three years. Do you think I have nothing better to do?" barked another. Usually, however, conductors leave the rejection routine to their secretaries or assistants. Some do not answer letters at all. Neither their contracts nor their careers require it.

On the other hand, an unwilling, cursory, or ill-prepared orchestral *première* can be worse than none at all. For, what work can survive a poor presentation? The public will be sure to ascribe the failure to the work alone; and very often the composer is so demoralized by this that he, too, blames himself.

Well then, has a conductor no obligations toward the living

writers, merely because their existence poses problems familiar to every political officeholder? H. L. Mencken who, as is well known, was a man of wide musical culture, was constrained to write: "The worst curse of music in this great Republic, it seems to me, is the foreign conductor. Nine times out of ten he is a plain mountebank, and the tenth he is hardly more than a propagandist for European music." While Mr. Mencken's arithmetic has in it an element of dramatic license, his sentiments are nevertheless not to be ignored. Plainly, he was referring to the conductor of the big orchestras. I am certain that if an American were permitted to hold a regular conductorial post of importance in a foreign country (which has never yet been known to happen), and would there exhibit the indifference or condescension toward that country's musical authors and performers that is accepted and even approved here as the correct thing, it would only be a matter of weeks before he would be asked to account for his actions to our State Department.

Polite circles are against doing anything about all this. To speak patriotically in music is today subversive, nay, treasonable. "We must have the highest standards. We want only quality." I grant that America has not yet developed the equal of Toscanini in conducting. But I say it never will, unless we admit our talent to the paths up Parnassus. I will gladly settle for the second-best in the interim, knowing we will presently match anything the modern world has to offer. But I have little faith in any reforms instituted through the practiced old hands that have made a bank out of our music.

In fairness it must be added, however, that the European conductor in this country is making some valuable and often brilliant contributions in the collegiate opera field, in which our native conductors have had as yet only limited experience. In some universities[1] one can see student productions that could be put on the boards of the professional opera houses abroad

[1] I name but a few of which I have had some personal experience: University of California at Los Angeles, University of Southern California, Indiana, Louisiana, and Columbia Universities, Hunter College, and conservatories like New England and Juilliard.

with real distinction. I doubt if Europe could match these standards on the academic level; the significant difference is that here the singers pay in order to participate, while abroad they are paid—an odd circumstance in view of the respective wealth represented. Unquestionably opera has found its only real home in America on the campus. But in our enthusiasm over this new development, we are apt to forget that this does not provide a profession for singers, and only a limited one for conductors. Nor does it offer them the variety and experience needed for the top reaches of the art.

In contrast, we cannot fail to see that some Americans, when they do achieve prominent conducting responsibilities, tend to imitate certain of the less salutary traits of their colleagues from abroad, even outdoing them in snobbery, pedantry, exhibitionism, not to say acquiescence toward the imitative and cautious taste of those who control orchestra policy. This may be a mark of insecurity, but may also suggest that they were chosen for their talents of conformance, rather than for their enterprise, stature, and independent spirit.

Very often we find that Europeans understand our desire for self-realization better than our compatriots. But then the development of generosity and insight, no less than enterprise, requires a modicum of success. We cannot expect a flowering of such qualities on a diet of lean opportunity.

The art is not to be compared to football; but it could learn something about its place in society from this sport in its earlier phases at least—a sport that grew out of the grammar and high schools, the colleges, the parks and the streets. Football would soon die if its activity were confined to the Big Leagues. If it continues to thrive it is because the game is played with fervor and conviction at all levels. Perhaps it too will soon go the way of music. In music there is left only the one Big League. The rest is like the Owens Valley of California, once a fertile land, but now reduced to sagebrush again, all its water having been impounded by the thirsty city of Los Angeles.

American music has not even the vitality to put up a real

fight for itself. "If the American musicians had only the vigor of its businessmen," cried Bloch once, "then we would soon see something!" But they have (to paraphrase Sinclair Lewis) cultivated caution until they have lost the power to be interested. Our music is a frustrated mendicant standing hat in hand watching the Occupation's Parade, nodding to organized power, and cheering as loudly as is expected. It is, aside from its repressive centralization, clique-ridden, dominated by perverse tendencies, and plainly lacking in self-respect.

I do not say the composer must necessarily organize against these conditions. I only say he should *live* against them, whatever that way of living may be: whether as teacher, writer, singer, player, conductor, scholar, or critic. And if he is a citizen in the American tradition, he will extend the hand of hospitality to all worthy comers from the world over, but *he will not therefore give up his place.* He will include himself.

The Experimental View

Though music is never pure mechanics, the musical author will sometimes resort to mechanical devices to recover his spirit. Music does not always begin with a feeling. It may be sparked by some technical experiment, into which a feeling then enters. An intellectual delight springs from the discovery of something ingenious or novel, which is not always possible to distinguish from a sense of beauty. The important thing is to get the blood flowing, the excitement going—to invoke the prescience of something about to happen. I suspect that few discoveries took place without some gleam of forefeeling, or foreknowledge, which acts like the pilot fish leading the shark.

There is a story about Rossini with a gushing lady who kept troubling him as to how he arrived at his extraordinary fertility of ideas. Rossini replied by asking her to jab away, blindfolded, with her hatpin, at a piece of manuscript paper which he moved slowly about in front of her, and then proceeded to connect the various resulting perforations into a sensible melody, to which he very naturally added an accompaniment. It illustrates what every composer knows: namely that *any* combination of notes, rhythms, or chords can be made to make sense. Nearly every writer has at some period attempted the mechanical rearrange-

ment of the elements of his art through permutation, combination, and various contrapuntic and instrumental devices, if only
to seek the organic out of the adventitious.[1] But he does this
mainly with the hope of derutting himself, shedding his routine,
hoping to glimpse new vistas and garner new thoughts from the
jungle of the fortuitous. He looks about him like the painter
whose most inviting subjects are often the unplanned groupings
of houses and streets in our cities and who prefers these urban
wildernesses to its planned public squares, parks, and civic
centers, those naïve monuments to the expensive lyricism of
civic corruption.

In the end, order comes out of chaos, the organic emerges
from brute stone, and all is humanized. "Good art," as Toch
remarks, "is the kind of art in whose center stands *man*."

But let us now regard music briefly from the mechanically
mutational standpoint. With our twelve equal notes of the
octave I have found it possible to construct precisely *350 separate
and distinct harmonies* (barring inversions, transpositions, and
varieties of open and close position), making it possible to form
1,469,650 different progressions of but two successive harmonies,
or over 6,000,000,000 progressions of three successive harmonies.
We can also make out of this same chromatic system some 1,490
scales, none of which employ an interval larger than the largest
used in the harmonic minor scale, namely, the augmented second.
If we were to go into quarter-tones or sixth-tones, as Busoni
once suggested, then these figures would swell to even more
indigestible dimensions.[2]

[1] The examples are endless. One cannot overlook Bach's almost invariable
practice of rearranging his voices in his fugues, or his ingenious permutations of
chord notes in his preludes; or Beethoven's tireless experiments with chord positions, open and close; or Chopin's fertile experiments with piano figurations,
never two alike. Perhaps it is the permutative tendency in composing that accounts
for the popular saying that music and mathematics are close to each other. Otherwise there is little foundation for this common belief, composers being notoriously
unmathematical—unless, as Professor Pace suggests, music and mathematics are
two *arts* in which original work has often been done at a very early age.

[2] See Ernst Bacon, "Our Musical Idiom," in *The Monist*, October, 1917;
Ferruccio Busoni, *A New Esthetic of Music* (New York: Schirmer Co., 1911).

This all looks very hopeful. But, as in our modern space explorations, we find the habitable planets to be few. The possibilities suggested through harmony are deceptive. Actually our chief vocabulary until the turn of the century centered around only a few simple chords. Most of our hymns use no more than the major and minor triads along with sometimes a seventh-chord.[3] Add to this the diminished and augmented chords and perhaps two or three seventh-chords, along with appogiaturas, suspensions, anticipations, passing and pedal notes, and you have a vocabulary that embraces most music up to the turn of the century. Even with these very limited means some entirely original music could be, and is, written today. Whatever goes beyond them has the appearance of being fashioned in large part out of these same simplicities, overlaid with other secondary elements. Probably what is most disturbing in our very recent music is that it limits itself almost wholly to these secondary elements, that is, to the superstrata.

There is in harmony something fundamental that corresponds to the three primary colors. To say that it is the relation between tonic, dominant, and subdominant (or supertonic), each with its overtones, may be stretching the analogy beyond proper limits. Nevertheless, there is a corresponding effect between the mixing of primary colors and the mixing of such primary musical chords. The secondary colors, in turn thus obtained, will when further mixed, result in tertiary colors, all progressively tending toward the use of the full chromatic scale in all its infinite variety of invertive and sonorous distributions. This parallels the arrival at the various shades of gray through the successive mixing of pigments. The point is that as these tonal, as well as pigmental, colors are more and more mixed, their differentiation diminishes, and they tend to recede toward a horizon of near-indistinguishability.

[3] We need not minimize the possibilities of even so simple a vocabulary as this. For example, it is possible to make 12,167 different progressions of but four chords in succession using only the major and minor triads (not counting transpositions or inversions).

Thus it can be said that out of the 350 harmonies of our twelve-tone system, the overwhelming majority fall into this realm of near-indistinguishability. As harmony moved away from tonality, through the successive stages of chromaticism, the whole-tone scale, the eight-tone (two diminished sevenths) scale, the various superpositions of fourths, and finally the austere twelve-tone-row —while new colors were constantly revealed—the direction was necessarily toward nebulousness rather than brilliance. Thus the search for new color leads ultimately to no color at all.

Harmonic research has run into a cul-de-sac.[4] Melody has for a long time been reduced to a servitude of harmony and instrumentation. Counterpoint, while it should be a discipline toward flexibility of melody, has become, instead, a cloak wherewith to conceal in its intricacy what amounts to a melodic and rhythmic paucity.

If we are to pioneer in newer areas of musical thought, our attention should now be turned less toward harmony; and we should perhaps temper our uses of, and demands upon, polyphony. In this connection, it could be said that Mozart and Schubert often showed their understanding of counterpoint by using it sparingly.

Better fields await us elsewhere. There is, for instance, rhythm —in which the American has a singular advantage over continentals, enjoying more freedom from the old four-square tendencies through his dance and earlier folk music. As an example, the six-eight bar alone allows for 3,364 different rhythmic arrangements, using no note smaller than the sixteenth.[5] The bar of three-four has the same number of possibilities. The bar of four-

---

[4] Hindemith justly says: "If anything seems to be of little reward, it is the search for originality in harmony." He goes on to say, "We may ask whether we could not assemble chords novel in their succession (even if not in their individual arrangement of tones) to produce less traditional patterns of sound. Would not such novelty in succession be proof of a further extensibility of the harmonic material?"

[5] The half-bar unit of three-eighths may have 29 combinations and permutations. Each of these may either begin or end with a tie, or both. Each of these may be set against any one of the 29 patterns in the second half of the bar, making a total of 3,364 rhythmic possibilities.

four offers, obviously, a far greater variability. The possibilities with irregular bars so common with the Elizabethans are no less inviting, and lend themselves particularly well to recent poetry, of which there is so much that is metrically irregular.

The further exploitation of polyharmony, polytonality, and polyrhythm need not be dwelt on: they have been widely dealt with.

The study of new scales as a basis for harmonic and melodic thought, as formulated with exhaustive clarity by Slonimsky,[6] is an inviting field. Slonimsky offers a thorough-going analysis of sequence possibilities. By now we have probably recovered from the interdict laid on the sequence by the "lost-generation" theorists, and rediscovered the age-old fact that all music of the last three centuries uses sequence liberally; there is not a page of *The Well-tempered Clavichord* without it.

Through the use of melodic, rhythmic, and agogic elements taken from old dance and folk music, it is possible to arrive at a living use of archaic modality. A change of this kind, however simple, may take prolonged acclimatization.

Then there is unharmonized melody: "Not melody which wants to be harmonized, nor melody which achieves harmonic sense by draughtsmanship," to quote Tovey, "but the austere achievement, far more difficult than any atonality, of a melody that neither needs nor implies harmony." In other words, a return to pure musical drawing.

Despite the gloomy verdicts of more than one of our musical coroners, that the subject is beyond resuscitation—is in fact dead —much is still to be done with chromatic harmony. Bernhard Ziehn's *Manual of Harmony*, published near the turn of the century in Milwaukee, and possibly the most original theoretical work written in America, has a wealth of highly *inobsolete* suggestions, some of which have fallen on readier ears abroad than at home. Busoni referred his students often to Ziehn and treated him with profound respect.

[6] Nicolas Slonimsky, *Thesaurus of Scales and Melodic Patterns* (New York: Coleman-Ross Co., 1947).

The Orientals can teach us much as they taught the painters a century ago: their modes, moods, austerities, uses of the voice, absence of harmony often, instruments—above all, the percussions. We can learn economy from our folk music—the kind that has not submitted to the Broadway cult.[7]

After all these experimentations, the composer tends often to overstress the need for *variety*. The commonest fault today is diversity to the point of monotony, compactness to the point of turgidity. Variety is at its best coming out of continuity. A little of the sunshine of simplicity should help us find our way out of those dark Amazonian recesses, where we have been gloomily speculating on anti-tonality, anti-harmony, anti-melody, anti-romanticism, and the like. The improvisational excesses of the late "romantic" music have understandably become a weariness. Nevertheless, it is to be noted that many today who are loudest in condemning what they call "romanticism," seem to wallow most deeply in those subjective excesses they consider characteristic of that era. Who knows but the next generation will find the current cerebrations on structure, form, polyphony, and dissonant harmony no less wearisome, in addition to being pretentious. If performing outlets were not so tightly sealed, we could doubtless better shed the oppressive cloak of responsibility under which we stagger when we must crowd so much thought into the brief and expensive minutes allotted the composer nowadays. Freedom is needed, and above all, freedom to perform and free-

[7] Some scholars have the idea that folk music is a rather sorry vestige of the musical Victorian age. "Yes, Dvorak, Smetana and Grieg used to do this, and Liszt. But it's an outworked device." What then of De Falla, Bartok, Vaughan Williams, Copland, Villa-Lobos, Chavez, and Stravinsky? Indeed, it would be difficult to single out a composer of stature who did not at some time delve into the people's music, study its colors and contours, learn from it the natural use of language; above all, learn how to sing from the untaught singers. What finer tribute to the Hungarian Gypsy than the Liszt Rhapsodies? Or could Mozart, Schubert, Weber, and Brahms have written songs which have become accepted as German folk songs (a high compliment) had they not been steeped in their idiom? George Pullen Jackson says: "Great periods in the art of any ordinary people are those in which its gifted creators are in closest harmony with the genius of their race. . . . Its barren periods are those when the masters have been faithless to their own and have sought afar the good which lies so near."

dom too from those zealots who have of late imprisoned us in their penitentiary of musical reforms. "Freedom," also as Mr. Goldovsky so admirably stated at Tanglewood, "to make mistakes." Today a mistake is so costly that the culprit is hustled off to serve a life sentence in obscurity for a passing ineptitude. This practice, as Goldovsky pointed out, was not the school by which Wagner, Verdi, and Beethoven learned their art.

As in architecture we now return to the simplest geometric forms, so in music let us essay the starkest mathematic designs, the boldest sequences, imitations, and contraries, permutations and combinations, the purest lines and angles, the simplest of curves; let us translate the visual grandeur of geology into melodies. But if these fail to dance and sing, and merely crawl and wriggle, then into the ash can they must go. Let the American composer look for idioms that express the cut of life, the posture of athletics, the feel of democratic society, the temper of climate, the forms of worship, the materialism, the rhythm of language, poetry and prose, the romantic facts of history, and all that makes a piece of striped bunting seem to float a certain way in a particular wind. Let there be plenty of technique and engineering behind all this, but little "showing-off" of theories and devices.

We have had enough of problems. It is time for some resounding solutions.

On Originality

The highest praise that is ordinarily bestowed on a new work today is to call it original. It goes with an age of scientific discovery, to believe that artists, no less than those who conduct researches in medicine, physics, and chemistry, must make it their main business to invent, or discover (the distinction is often hazy) something heretofore unknown or unused. This is not entirely new. Composers of the last century also put a high premium on novelty, above all Berlioz and Liszt. But their age, which we like to call "romantic" was more charitably disposed than ours toward writers whose originality was incidental rather than deliberate. It honored Verdi, Mendelssohn, Tschaikovsky, and Brahms no less than those who were looked upon as "pioneers." It was satisfied if music had life and poetry. *Personality* was more esteemed than novelty.[1] It is a curious anomaly that as personality fades (and has it not faded? Where are the great personalities of music since Strauss, Mahler, Busoni, Paderewski, Rachmaninoff, Kreisler, Toscanini?) the general level of technical accomplishment rises, and with this rise we become sharper and

---

[1] This is not to say that competence has declined. On the contrary, virtuosos are to be found in every field, not singly but in platoons. It would seem, however, that precision and accomplishment have replaced individuality. Perhaps, to paraphrase Thoreau, it is for want of an Artist that there are so many artists.

84

more detective-minded in our appraisals. Knowledge has replaced insight.

In view of all this, the public taste has not been altered as much as is supposed since then. Witness only the predominance of nineteenth-century music on our current programs. Nevertheless, the theorists and critics exercise a greater sway over our opinions than they ever have before. All music is accessible to them now through records (all, that is to say, except some of the very best American music of our time), and there is no more fashionable pastime than the ferreting out of influences, resemblances and hidden quotations. This tune and harmony-sleuthing is, of course, on an essentially literal level, and rarely touches on what is meant or said.[2]

Unhappily for those who write today, resemblances are re-garded as no less blameworthy in the present than praiseworthy in the past. We get very legal about it all, and put up "No Tres-passing" signs all over the place. Too bad the dead cannot profit by our conscientious scruples over their posthumous patent rights. There is no doubt that a great deal of recent music has undergone minute alteration, subtraction and addition, with nothing more in mind than a clouding of such resemblances. It has led to what some innocents call the "wrong note" school, which prescribes that you write a tune with normal harmonies and then doctor these up to the point where the distortions will pass for learned modernisms. Whoever has learned the grammatical way finds it easy enough to deviate from it, just as learning to spell teaches how to misspell, if we think it worthwhile to do so. It does not follow that this practice is necessarily dishonest craftsmanship, but it calls to mind that there were times when there were no strictures on borrowing, when unconventional writing was as much censured as we today censure conventional writing.

The line of demarcation between allowable borrowing and plagiarism has never been clear. Every great maker of verse,

---

[2] Brahms met the charge of plagiarism with the famous retort, "Every ass can see that!" Gounod gave a more polished rejoinder, "You cannot imagine how flattered I am to be reminded that certain phrases of mine remind you of Mozart."

music, sculpture, or painting discovers at some time that he may not only borrow, but *must* borrow, in making a work of larger dimensions. Would it be possible to construct a new house, however original, without using some standard materials, most of which could be labeled with the name of their inventor or manufacturer? It is mostly the nonproductive persons who fail to realize this need for appropriation. The artist, who ought to know the laws of parentage, should be the first to deny exclusive patents in art. "Your business," said Swift, "is not to steal from the ancients but to improve upon them and make their sentiments your own." The builder cannot afford to be as fastidious as the commentator.

But to borrow successfully from a known model, it is necessary to surpass the model in quiddity, and to shed on it the light of new meaning. For example, Beethoven's theme opening the slow movement of the *Sonata Pathétique* begins identically with a secondary subject of the slow movement of Mozart's sonata in the same key. This is borrowing beyond cavil, whether awarely or not. Yet Beethoven invests the melody with a new importance and gravity, puts it in the forefront, and carries it to an entirely different completion, making it indisputably his own. With Mozart, the idea was distinctly subordinate; and were we to interpolate in its stead what Beethoven did with the same, his entire movement would suffer dislocation. One could add, that were Beethoven a minor personage in history, his use of Mozart's idea would probably be condemned as a plagiarism. So we may say *that the recognized writer absorbs the work of others, while the unrecognized writer steals it.* The rich in reputation, like the rich in possessions, are likely to have less trouble with the law.

In turn, Beethoven, one of music's most daring and tireless explorers, threw out original suggestions lavishly in the course of his later writings, to which nearly every composer of the nineteenth century was indebted; passages which, in their context, he gave little further development, but whose essence is discoverable in the works of most of the later masters. Every generation exploits the legacy of ideas given it by the previous one, and leaves to the next its own legacy of ideas not fully explored. Nor need a parent, in art as in life, bewail the insufficient gratitude of his offspring. For the child will in turn pay the debt he owes his parents to his own children. "It is with books as with the fires in our grates," says Voltaire. "Everybody borrows a light from his neighbor to kindle his own, which in its turn is communicated to others, and each partakes of all."

Of two streams uniting, the lesser one is called the tributary. The river's name goes to the fuller stream. We call our greatest river the Mississippi, and not the Missouri, though the sources of the latter are a great deal farther from their confluence at St. Louis. Thus we credit Wagner with the name of the musical stream that had its tributaries in Weber, Liszt, and Berlioz. The merging German and Italian streams in Handel and Bach flow on henceforward as German. The calculus goes to Newton rather than to Leibnitz (at least in English-speaking countries), while the theory of natural selection goes to Darwin rather than Wallace.

But the search for the absolute beginning of any school or tendency in art proves invariably futile. A true originality would probably prove to be a mutational monstrosity. Whenever a work or its author are pronounced uniquely individual, examination will show that the sources have simply not been made known. Every woodsman knows how deceptive the search for a stream's source can be. He finds what appears to be the ultimate spring, only to discover, as he goes higher up, a series of waterholes. And where indeed does the water begin: on the hillsides, in the trees, in the sky, or in the distant sea? What we should properly seek instead of this chimerical thing, originality, is *personality*, which could be likened to some great feature in the course of a stream, like a waterfall, a gorge, a lake, a shoal, or again a mill-dam—the same stream flowing on through all.

In studying the masterpieces of the past, one is struck with two things. The first is their essential similarity in basic thought, the second is their freshness of statement. Great music or great poetry always gives one, even at first hearing, an impression of familiarity. But there is about it also that pristine quality of a first discovery. This is because the relation of old wisdom to new experience must be new and unprecedented. Ancient man, and new times, will always produce a new counterpoint.

There is a kind of family inheritance in the arts. It shows itself on various levels. There are those who inherit the grand tradition: the large builders, the integraters; and there are those who have a tendency to seek out novelty above all: the experimenters. Occasionally they unite in one personality, as in Beethoven. But it is a mistake to assume that the two must be coincidental. The complete artist does not seek out novelty or experiment unless he is driven to it by larger plans. "Bach," says Schweitzer, "belongs to the order of objective artists who are wholly of their time, and feel no inner compulsion to open new paths." "I have not attached the least value to the discovery of a novelty," said Gluck, "unless naturally suggested by the situation and wedded to its expression." Tschaikovsky had long been charged with failing to invent new musical idioms. His nationalist *confrères* of Balakirev's persuasion considered him a musical Germanophile. But he felt no call to invent new idioms, nor to nationalize himself in Russian folklore or ancient church music as did Moussorgsky. Tschaikovsky, educated in the German tradition, grew *into* the ground like a transplanted cutting; Moussorgsky, instead, grew *out* of it as from a seed. What is important to us of today is that both grew superbly tall and left us the most glorious musical fruits of their time and place. Nor could it be said that Tschaikovsky's music has for us of today any the less stamp of personality, or of Russianism, than has the music of Moussorgsky—even though the latter's originality is incomparably the greater. It has taken educated musicians three generations to discover the full stature of Tschaikovsky which, oddly enough, the unsophisticated public recognized from the very first.

"If you ask what innovations the hitherto greatest musical genius, Mozart, introduced," remarks Ernst Toch, "the answer can only be, none whatsoever. He accepted the musical status of his age as it was passed on to him, he used the forms as his predecessors evolved them, kept within the tonal and harmonic confines of the epoch. All this has not limited him, has not prevented him from erecting within this frame the edifice of a work comparable to none before him or after, merely by the inexhaustibility of his inspiration."

"Contemporary" music has its fashions, which are no less variable than the styles of ladies' hats. The arrival of every new prophet of sound on our shores, with attendant fanfare, is followed by a wave of imitations, most of which are scarcely distinguishable from their original. However, since musical habits last longer than clothes, there ensues a greater overlapping of styles. The resultant confusion defies analysis. Certain it is, nevertheless, that a great deal that passes for original is sheerest counterfeit. Indeed, *the surest way to achieve a reputation for originality is to copy the newest fashions in sound.* The reviewer of today must have the greatest difficulty distinguishing the integrity of musical objects when all are so intermixed in style, not to say so thickly overlaid with polyphonic or cacophonic mud.

It is interesting to note how many of those who strive to be unique sound alike.

No doubt, in much of this music, the art follows some special definition, and thus it appears to realize its own time, out of which such theories have sprung. Instead, as Wilde said, "The definition should follow the work," to which he adds, "Those who advise you to make your art representative of the century are advising you to produce an art which your children will think old-fashioned."

With all its uses and pleasures, jazz is more symptom and pastime than imperishable utterance

JACQUES BARZUN

Jazz

It is often asked, what role will jazz play in the serious music of the future? The probable reply is that jazz, like any kind of popular, folk, or less sophisticated music (as distinguished from what we so condescendingly call "art music") will find its way into the larger music as did the waltz, the polonaise, the minuet, the gigue, the sarabande, or the folk song, in the past. This seems quite obvious, and, of course, the reverse as well, namely that popular strains absorb the sophisticate music in course of time. But now Henry Pleasants says in *The Agony of Modern Music*,[1] "Jazz *is* modern music, and nothing else is." The interloper has become the proprietor. Mr. Pleasants demonstrates with uncommon brilliance what a morass most contemporary "serious" music has run into, and from this makes a bravura leap to the conclusion that "the evolution of Western music continues in American popular music," even dragging Europe along. While Mr. Pleasants may not have meant it this way, his expression will most certainly appeal to all the "Bach to bebop" enthusiasts and will raise a great shout of triumph from the bobby-soxers. It has a patriotic note too, for what could be as native and "democratic" as jazz? There is no doubt that our jazz has been seized upon by the youth

[1] New York: Simon and Schuster, 1955.

90

of many lands, and has in fact become a symbol of the youth movement.

Few musicians of culture today will slur or belittle jazz, and everyone knows that a vigorous exchange of techniques and viewpoints between its devotees and the symphonists has long been taking place, whether we look in Ravel, Stravinsky, Rachmaninoff, Britten, or Copland, or else in Gershwin, Rodgers, Ellington, Brubeck, or Jamal. But a total surrender to Mr. Pleasants' thesis could well prove to be as unfair to the one party as to the other. Surely the jazz men would not wish, nor be prepared, to assume symphonic responsibilities any more than the symphonists would care to assume the burdens of popular entertainment in this day of universal restlessness, when music has assumed the main burden of distraction, of diffusing the world's tensions and fears (some of which it may even be a party to generating). We doubt if the youth movement is being well served by Mr. Pleasants' compliment.

Youth movements are no less often bad than good. The world, in its reasonable periods, has acknowledged age's claims as well as those of youth, realizing that youth will never understand age, while age will seldom remember youth. What is meant is that youth (and jazz *is* youth, if anything is), should not presume, or be encouraged, to speak for maturity. For example, I will not say what music young people should enjoy—but have they the right to subject me in every public place to a jazz bath? I do not mean that I want "classical" music in restaurants, railroad stations, toilets, department stores, and airplanes. *I want no music at all,* outside my musical devotions, and ought to have the same right to silence as they have to noise. After all, my quiet makes no inroads on them save that it imposes certain restraints of a kind we recognize in all other walks of life. The abuse of these restraints is, of course, not to be laid, in fairness, at the doorstep of jazz alone, nor even of its maudlin cousin, "popular music." It is a business—and a very big business at that, mostly run for and by substantial middle-aged men—that places the instruments of aural tyranny in public places, where they can then be thoughtlessly used, to the discomfiture and misery of a large portion of the population that has long been reduced to a state of numb acquiescence.

Jazz has its own special sphere, that of a unique kind of intoxication and parody. It says, in effect, "Get off your high horse and mix with the gang." Despite its fastidious moments, it is for the most part blatantly and outrageously democratic and proletarian. Gershwin said, "It is the result of energy stored up in America . . . noisy, boisterous and vulgar." Surely it embodies the most engaging vulgarity of our day, perhaps the only vulgarity to which one may subscribe, for it makes an art out of vulgarity itself and thus comes clean—that is to say, the real jazz, not the manufactured stuff, the synthetic "drip" that feeds the insatiable maw of radio, television, and Musak.

But can anyone imagine jazz in sacred music? Does it speak of the feelings out of which any great music has been made before, or is perhaps the impulse toward great music no more alive today? Can it evoke the qualities of heroism, splendor, devotion, tenderness, romantic love, or aspiration? Can it build grand symphonic or choral monuments? Can it speak of sorrow, deprivation, despair, or death? Can it touch on any of these with more than a note of travesty, or a grimace? "I doubt," remarked Ortega, "that any young person of our time can be impressed by a poem, a painting, or a piece of music that is not flavored with a dash of irony." Insofar as jazz is the supreme music of irony in our day, one must grant its supremacy over serious music on this ground, and agree with Mr. Pleasants. But will you have it in your cathedrals, at your weddings, or at solemn occasions? Will you allow the juke box to become your altar?

Perhaps a recent experiment with a folk Mass or so-called Jazz Mass by the Rev. Geoffry Beaumont will revise our estimate. Meanwhile the Rev. Kendall Edkins remarks of it: "There are elements of both [jazz and folk music] in addition to operetta music, Hollywood musical, plainchant, and extravaganza. . . . If the Lord's Prayer is to be sung to syncopated rhythm, let it be honestly and consistently done, not dressed up for church with a phoney introduction."

Then, too, granted all the abuses to which recent "serious" musical thinking may have led, in creating obscure, crabbed, long-winded, and sometimes ill-mannered and offensive music, are we therefore ready to give up our taste for large and involved musical structure? For in this jazz could play at best a contributing role. "An entire composition written in jazz could not live," said Gershwin. Recognizing that jazz may have had some development since his time, that still does not make it a bedfellow of the sonata, the fugue, the symphony, the opera, or the tone poem; nor can we with honesty say these larger forms have spent themselves. Consider only the limitations it suffers (or enjoys) in its inflexible, monotonous beat, its absence of rubato, its small vocabulary of harmony, its melodic paucity. Sometimes the pretensions of the jazz purists (and who can be more "pure"?) remind one a little of the pretensions of the atonalists. Like Mr. Krenek, who says, "If thinkers can learn from this phenomenon [atonal music] the direction of the road leading to the world music, then the world will perhaps have derived from its catastrophe [World War I] the only tangible advantage accessible to it today." We are reminded of the Thirties when it became fashionable in American intellectual circles to decry our Jeffersonian politics as something outworn that must soon give way to the deeper truths of an economic materialism.

Nor is it necessary to look on the improvisational character of the jam session as something wholly unique. There are other improvising groups in the world, the Gypsies, for example. The jam session was a salutary reaction to the curbing of individual creative impulse by the fancy orchestrations of the large bands— started back in the Whiteman days. I am all for the jam session. It is jazz at its very best. But the history of music has yet to show an instance where any form of spontaneous group music-making can equal or surpass the organized creations of a single man of genius. Does not his genius lie in the power not only to hold the spontaneous inspiration of an improvised moment, but to enlarge, develop and perfect this, let alone make it literate and accessible to all that come after? Nearly all great composers improvised. But they knew also that, whatever spontaneity such made-on-the-spot music possessed, it could not bear closer examination subsequently. I have the greatest admiration for those rare few improvisers of our own time, who have retained that high art—men like the organist, DuPré, or the pianist, Templeton; but they do not need me to tell them that they are not creating immortal masterpieces with their extemporizings, brilliant as they are.

The morale of jazz is not a negligible factor in this comparison. Delius once said, "In an age of neurasthenics, music, like everything else, must be a stimulant, must be a alcoholic, aphrodisiac, or it is no good." If jazz has a supreme gift, it is that of breaking down inhibitions. Can anyone doubt that the better the bebop, or the rock 'n roll, the more is it conducive to orgiastic reactions? We are urged to believe then, because "serious" music has become too inhibited—for that is what the over-intellection amounts to—we should therefore cast in our unstinting lot with an art that cannot wholly deny its part in the present wave of juvenile and adult indecorum, even delinquency. How superbly it routs pretension and hypocrisy. But the raucous laugh or the ruttish joke it suggests, are these to be extolled? Some jazz is plain pornography, often outrageously funny, but certainly not appropriate just anywhere.

In giving jazz the present-day crown, we should also not overlook the handicap our "serious" American music has suffered because of its ingrained habit of dependence on Europe. It is still being taught with a foreign accent, has never yet had its rightful innings. Jazz, instead, grew like our theatre, from the ground up —not from the top down—untrammeled with erudite and alien restraints, and passed naturally from adolescence into maturity as an art should properly do. "Serious" music in America is still hanging on to parental apron strings and had better give up these filial devotions before it falls irretrievably into middle-age decrepitude. I make no defense for the failure of the latter; and I acknowledge fully that jazz has become far and away the most authentic musical speech of America. The relative circumstance, however, cannot be overlooked in making a comparison. We like to say this is alive and that is dead; this has a future, that has none. Yet the history of criticism shows that predictions have failed and succeeded in equal measure, particularly when they come from sources of pure erudition. Such prophecies lie, so to speak, in the foothills of the art, not high enough to be among the main peaks, nor yet far enough away to see them in silhouette; and are an unreliable guide to the art's ultimate values.

And yet, when all is said, and we have stripped jazz of its intellectual and cultural pretenses, doubted its capacity to vie with the symphony, and acknowledged fully only its claim to the crown of parody and intoxicant irresponsibility, it remains the sprightliest musical child we have yet conceived. If it could shed its almost inseparable companion, the unspeakably tawdry and dull so-called "popular" music, and at the same time succeed in not wearing out its welcome with too immodest a ubiquity, it must win all hearts save the most philistine; for it has vitality and nativity. And as between too much of this with too little brains, and too much brains with too little vitality and nativity, the former has the better claim to art.

THE TEACHER

It takes two to speak the truth—one to speak, and another to hear.

HENRY DAVID THOREAU

The Interview

The modern student of composition comes to his teacher with the request: Let me learn from you all the modern techniques.

The teacher replies: Even if I knew them all, you could not possibly assimilate them, or fuse them into a homogeneous style. They are as diverse as the Chinese and Spanish languages. Your mind would become a hodge-podge.

The pupil rejoins: But I want to learn them all, so I can then decide which to keep and which to discard.

Teacher: You seem to regard these "techniques" as so many hats that you can try on and reject at will. Instead, each one, if studied properly, which involves an extended process of domestication, becomes in the end a habit and leaves its mark on your personality, which is to say, your style. *To learn is to experience.* It would be absurd for you to try to fortify your health by experiencing all known illnesses. Besides you can't sample everything. "It is only an auctioneer," was Wilde's famous apothegm, "who should admire all schools of art."

Student: What, then, am I to study?

Teacher: You can always study the classics, as have your predecessors, including those who have gone farthest afield later.

Student: That seems very limiting, and out of date.

99

Teacher: It is not limiting to study the works of the last six centuries, which include the greatest music we know, as compared to the works of but one or two recent generations. Some theorists seem to imagine that music has "progressed" with the same rapidity as the sciences. It may have tried to keep pace theoretically with science, but the public has little part in these new "experiments," and the public reaction is not to be despised. An artist, like a politician, may be ahead of his constituents in his thought, but *he cannot afford to sever himself* from them. He must stay in rhythm, even when he strains ahead. Beyond limits a man may not invent too many new symbols.

Student: Wasn't Beethoven in advance of his times?

Teacher: Indeed he was, but mostly in his late works, when he "lit out," you could almost say, to a land of no return; but that was when his deafness had already cut him off from society.

Student: But his earlier works were very daring and original too?

Teacher: That they were; yet he must have been an enormously popular man, when you consider that his funeral brought out a tenth of Vienna on a rainy day.

Student: Even if modern music has fallen short of its theoretical aims, can I ignore modern theories?

Teacher: You cannot ignore them. You cannot even escape them. They belong to your day and age no less than the theories of Marx, Freud, Einstein, and Spengler. They are part of it. But you must not believe that everything that goes on around you needs to go into your music. Some people do, of course. Others interpret their time by expressing how they as sensitive people react to all this, which is not necessarily in a spirit of uncritical acquiescence. I can't tell you how you are to react. I only say that the unpleasant noise in the sky at this particular moment, probably due to some low-flying helicopter or jet plane, is not the whole story of today. If you have a real bent for theory and mathematics you would be foolish to rule these out of your music. If you are of an opposite turn of mind you'd be equally foolish to try to incorporate them.

Student: I am not yet satisfied with what you have said to my question about being limited.

Teacher: It is your contemporaries who are the most likely to limit you. Nearly all of them, having in their day searched for new and arable lands to cultivate, have been intimidated from settling in the better bottomlands of the past by warning signs saying, "Posted." These signs were, however, seldom left by the artists of former days, who gave little thought to the patenting of their inventions. The signs were mostly put up by modern lawyers and legislators of beauty, for whom patents are a stock-in-trade, and who acknowledge only the novel and unheard-of in their time, and allow no poaching on familiar territory, though they are well-enough aware how many of their ancestors made their start in this very way. At any rate, the musical writers of today have generally sought out some remote area, often charming and fascinating, but seldom large enough to sustain more than themselves.

What profit can it be to you, then, to try to squeeze yet more out of such depleted resources, and to label yourself a follower of this or that man?

Besides, have you ever noticed that the original discoverers of new things in music almost invariably surpass those who follow in their footsteps? Here is where art is wholly unlike science or invention, in the course of which constant improvement actually does take place. In art, however, the first full-fledged statement of a new idea is generally the strongest. Take, for example, a few of the greatest innovators: say, Monteverde, Beethoven, Wagner, and Moussorgsky. Can you show me where any of these has been surpassed by a follower, as, let us say, Lamarck was by Darwin, Planck by Einstein, Lilienthal by the Wrights? The distinction lies in that the personality of an automobile's manufacturer, scientist or even inventor is of secondary moment as compared to the car itself, the invention or the discovery, while the personality of a composer is the very essence of his work.

The classics are to be studied. The moderns you will absorb, whether you try or not, to the extent that they attract you.

Student: How then, may I achieve variety?

Teacher: There is little danger of your music not having sufficient variety. Modern music is choked with variety. Composers
of today pack their scores with far too many and diverse elements. With performances so rare and costly, they attempt to
say a great many things, in a period of time that allows for only
very few. It makes for a disparity between the tempo of presentation and the tempo of assimilation. The listener cannot follow the lecturer. Between unity and variety runs a very delicate
line of balance, to follow which is the mark of a developed taste.
It is perhaps better to err with excessive uniformity than with
excessive variety.

Student: Can you give me some basis of procedure, then?

Teacher: Your chief concern, in this day of artistic anarchy,
is to search out your own likes (a difficult task demanding much
lonely labor and meditation) and to develop them to the point
where you can present them with conviction. You will then be
understood, and will not be a useless counterfeit of someone else.
The important thing is not to expect to begin on this labor of
self-discovery with a ready formula. The formula will probably
not disclose itself to you until you have done enormous labors.
And this same process is apt to repeat itself all your life—that is,
if you will not allow yourself to be content with saying the same
thing over and over again, as others will usually expect and even
pay you to do. The goal should always advance with the achievement. This is why even Haydn found it no easier to compose in
ripest maturity than in youth, or why Wagner struggled more to
write *Parsifal* than *The Flying Dutchman*.

The most original of modern poets said, in his late years, "My
verdict and conclusions as illustrated in *Leaves of Grass* are
arrived at through the temper and inculcation of the *old works*
as much as through anything else."

Student: You have made your advice persuasive. I will think
it over carefully, and at the next opportunity tell you to what
extent I feel it possible to follow it.

Teacher: I expect nobody to accept my advice. I am better

complimented if it stimulates you to thought rather than acquiescence. Since there are few matters in which I find it possible to agree with prevalent opinion, however, I thought it worthwhile to give you my views. In the end it will not be *reason* that decides for you, but *inclination*, and that is as it should be.

Student: Now I would like, with your permission, to ask a few questions of a more academic sort. I have to consider how I will make my living after graduation. I have no illusions about a virtuoso career.

Teacher: As a matter of fact, from what I've heard, you could become a first-rate pianist. But first you have to consider the problem of money to finance yourself until you have made a name. Careers are rarely made on merit alone. Then, if you do succeed in making a name, you will discover that the world exacts of you *all or nothing*. You will either give a hundred concerts a year, or none. No large management will invest money—your money of course—in you, and not exploit you to the full. So you will have remaining at best the summers to write in, when, by all rights, you should be practicing for the next season.

Student: I had thought rather to make teaching my livelihood.

Teacher: This, too, you should only do if you have a real inclination toward it. Too many go into teaching because of the "security" it promises (that is, particularly the public-school field). The art of teaching deserves to be served by something better than a corps of professional frustrates. I have seen on the bulletin boards of more than one college advertisements that shamelessly try to lure the student into "music education" on the grounds that a guaranteed job awaits them with the music education degree. Fortunately, our liberal arts courses have not yet stooped to advertising themselves as guarantees of job success.

Student: I don't suppose that a secondary school would be a very good place for a man who wants to write.

Teacher: So far it has not proven to be. Its policies are almost as rigid as its schedules. Your associations would not always be stimulating. Yet, I don't see why the direction of a high school chorus couldn't be very rewarding. Boys and girls at that age have a tremendous vitality, and the quality of their voices can be exquisite. Orchestras pose a bigger problem, because the strings are so widely neglected today. Bands, again, are better, except for their limited literature, for the winds are simpler to learn; then too there are all the allurements of uniforms, athletic games, and so on. The worst thing about the public schools is their approach to music, which is seldom on an artistic level, and which has been formulated between music educators and the state legislators to serve all levels, which can mean in practice only the lowest. That special legally ordained degree, which entails a routine of "education" courses that are mostly the apogee of boredom and unmusicality, yet without which a Mozart wouldn't be entrusted with a class in a public school, requires the holder to have studied such a variety of things that he usually knows almost nothing about any one of them. It encourages what amounts to a versatility of ignorance. The emphasis is more on *how* to teach than on acquiring *something worth teaching*. Method triumphs over matter. The late Pope Pius XIII, while yet a cardinal, visited the United States, and being interested in education, was shown one of our great teachers' seminaries, where the new emphasis on "method" prevailed. "I feel very old-fashioned," he is reported to have said. "In my time the main qualification for a teacher was that he had mastered his subject." As a result, most instruments and singing are not only poorly taught in the public schools, but the teacher has also never had time or inducement to know *music* itself.

The wonder is that the children play as well individually as they do in their school bands; but the quality of their concerted music is seldom distinguished, and very often in poor taste. There is no reason, particularly in the cities, why each instrument should not be properly taught by an expert, who could go about from school to school. Some cities have, in fact, already taken up this approach. I think it is important that children in their most impressionable years should be taught by persons of cultivated taste. The music they play can be as simple as you wish, and yet it must be good. One does not expect school children to become artists, but one has the right to expect they should be taught by artists. Does an art deserve any less? And surely it is not degrading for an artist to teach children. The degrading part is the conditions under which he must do it: the supervision by persons of unformed taste, the imposition of ill-advised curricula, and often the simple lack of decent equipment.

But we are digressing from your matter. Do you by any chance play the organ?

Student: I once studied the organ, but gave it up in favor of the piano. Now I am wondering if this was sensible.

Teacher: I would advise you, if you are not disinclined, to perfect yourself in this kingly instrument. Here is one realm in which real progress is being made. Everywhere, and particularly on college campuses, fine new organs are being installed by Holtkamp, Schlicker, Aeolian-Skinner and other good firms. The old movie-type organ that vainly attempted to be an orchestra has gone out. Instead we are now getting instruments that are made for the performance of the great organ literature. It is interesting that a new literature is now springing up in keeping not only with the new instruments but which does justice to the organists now developing everywhere in America, a group that takes second place to none. The churches have been revising their hymnals with better standards than have been current the last hundred years.

Student: This prospect is attractive; and I'm also enormously interested in the choral music that is possible in the churches.

Teacher: Aside from the song literature, the literature for chorus is the most neglected of all. We know only a handful of works by writers like Bach and Handel, and a few scattered works of the great earlier masters, Schütz, Monteverde, Josquin, Byrd, Lassus, Palestrina, Vittoria, and Alessandro Scarlatti. The choral works of even the later writers since Bach are only partially known. Compare this vastly neglected literature with the no-less overworked literature of the orchestra.

There is another good aspect to choral conducting. You are dealing mostly with amateurs who sing for pleasure, rather than with professionals who play for pay. You are not going to be penalized for your extra efforts to bring a work to perfection. The pay is small, and there is much elementary teaching to be done with most choruses, but the artistic rewards are high.

Student: I read in William Lyon Phelps' autobiography that he strongly advised writers to avoid a teaching career. Do you agree with him, apart from the factor of necessity?

Teacher: What he means, though I don't remember his words, is that a teacher can easily talk himself dry in lecturing; put into his teaching what ought to go into his work; waste his most precious secrets, acquired through the years, on students who are neither ready for them, nor indeed as yet worthy of them. Also, in a situation where his opinions are so little challenged, he may develop a dogmatic air, or else fall into a comfortable sluggishness in his labors, since he has the protection—once he has passed a certain barrier—of tenure. As between the complacency of most college music and the brawling contentiousness of professional music, I cannot say which is worse. In the one there is not enough competition; in the other there is too much.

Student: I remember hearing Rudolf Serkin saying to you, after he had just been concertizing all over the country, how he envied you the restful life of the college campus.

Teacher: I can understand him, considering that he said this in a moment of weariness with travel. But you should know that life such as we have here is almost monkish; the isolation is often unbearable. Provincial America, throughout which America's cultural centers are widely scattered, is socially and artistically repressive. Where there ought to be a community of creative people, there seldom is, and one must build the fire to warm the spirit entirely oneself (stop and think what that means). The dignity has gone out of the life of the professor, now that he is socially rated by his income, which, having never kept pace with rising costs, is a constant source of embarrassment; he is no longer, like his traditional predecessor, an urbane, traveled, gregarious, hospitable citizen; and his family suffers the effects of all this. Nevertheless, I must add that, having once accepted the conditions I describe, I still find many compensations in campus life. There is more time for personal work than in other occupations, if a man can effectively use it, that is to say, unfreeze himself; there are the students, perennially and irrepressively cheerful, and often eager; and there is the ivory tower that still survives the age of electronics and commercialized sex, and which, if anything, has gained a new dignity in its modern environment.

Student: Two years of college are left to me. In what do you advise me to concentrate most heavily?"

Teacher: I would study all the music theory that is offered, *provided it is well taught.* I made it a principle in my college days to give priority to the teacher over the subject. That is to say, I would settle for my second choice of subject with a first-rate teacher, over my first choice with a second-rate teacher. The good teacher, even though he produces nothing original, is a valuable asset to a school. Some years ago, Harvard University set an inordinately high premium on publication as evidence of original work and as a yardstick for promotion. The result was a deluge of publication. The all-out teacher, who may have developed lecturing to a finer art than research, was made to feel very insecure. Administrations make a mistake every time they try to "evaluate" people by any mechanical yardsticks, such as publication, activity in learned societies, honorary degrees, and the like. These, doubtless necessary, facets of the campus have become far too political. Pick your subjects with care. Pick your teachers with even greater care.

Student: When you spoke of music theory, why did you say nothing about "composition." Isn't that my first concern?

Teacher: I hope it is, and for this very reason you should guard it against the influence of false and unnecessary pedagogy. Have you ever heard of any poet having learned his art through courses in poetry writing? Courses in literature—yes, and in grammar and rhetoric—yes. A teacher of composition can give you advice; he can encourage you; he can praise you for good work; he can suggest that you try yourself out in some hitherto untried field; he can see that you get performed, when you've written something worth performing. He can correct grammatical errors; suggest books to read; help you develop as an executant artist with the classics; give you theoretical problems to solve. But he cannot make a composer of you, nor should he be encouraged to try. That is purely your private affair, and the more you keep it separate from credits and degrees, the better. Your composition teacher is, at his very best, an impresario. Has ever a better lesson in composition been given than Whitman describes in *Specimen Days:*

"I walk'd for two hours, of a bright sharp February mid-day twenty-one years ago, with Emerson, then in his prime, keen, physically and morally magnetic, arm'd at every point, and when he chose, wielding the emotional just as well as the intellectual. During those two hours he was the talker and I the listener. It was an argument-statement, reconnoitring, review, attack, and pressing home (like an army corps in order, artillery, cavalry, infantry), of all that could be said against that part (and a main part) in the construction of my poems, 'Children of Adam.' More precious than gold to me that dissertation—it afforded me, ever after, this strange and paradoxical lesson: each point of E.'s statement was unanswerable, no judge's charge ever more complete or convincing, I could never hear the points better put—and then I felt down in my soul the clear and unmistakable conviction to disobey all, and pursue my own way. 'What have you to say then to such things?' said E., pausing in conclusion. 'Only that while I can't answer them at all, I feel more settled than ever to adhere to my own theory, and exemplify it,' was my candid response. Whereupon we went and had a good dinner at the American House. And thence-forward I never waver'd or was touch'd with qualms (as I confess I had been two or three times before)."

Student: This was indeed a great lesson, even though it only fortified Whitman in his resolve not to follow it.

Teacher: It is also a lesson to us, showing how the significant illuminations in our progress come unexpectedly, and scarcely never in the course of any school routines. Music, like poetry, is not authored through admonition. It is only musical grammar that can be taught this way. And there's your *theory*.

Student: What other studies would you have me follow?

Teacher: I have mentioned to you before now that musical scholarship occupies a disproportionately large place in American college life. I do not therefore deplore it, however. For it breeds, and is bred by, a new kind of amateur who is interested in the musical literature through records and the radio, rather than by playing an instrument or singing. His is a passive sort of learning.

Musicology has an analogy to academic language study, if one omits from the latter the writing courses, and takes into account, further, that music is a language acquired mostly through conscious study, while English is first learned automatically in childhood. Aside from its reading and writing, music is probably better understood by the unlettered than is poetry, and certainly better than painting. There is a growing interest in its history, its personalities, its literature, and its purport. The modern musicologist, who is on fortunate rare occasions an artist as well, is better able to satisfy this interest than his predecessor, who was usually a practicing musician with but an amateur equipment as scholar and historian. The former's approach to music tends to become a more intellectual one, and has the more need therefore to examine the past. The musicologist's researches have properly opened our eyes to forgotten epochs and extended our musical horizon into antiquity by centuries. His position today is comparable to that of the philologist and the literary historian.

There have been bitter controversies about musicology. It seems to me that wherever it has disparaged or discouraged actual music-making, which it certainly has in some quarters, it deserves censure and ridicule; but wherever it has encouraged music, and widened its repertory, it deserves praise. On the whole, the musicologists are a rather brilliant group of people, and consequently their influence for good or bad is above average. Besides, they have captured the citadel of most of our liberal arts colleges. Today you have a better guarantee of an academic post by being an authority on the sixteenth century, than if you are a first-class pianist or composer. Not that I approve of this at all; but if a man has the scholarly credentials to get into a good college, he can trick the authorities, benevolently perhaps, and use his influence and knowledge toward making a real musical life there.

Beethoven has probably fared no worse than Shakespeare in our sanctuaries of erudition, where poetry is analyzed for its prose, and masterpieces are dissected, leaving the cadaverous fragments lying about. It's all a matter of who is in charge. Theorists, piano teachers, and critics are all guilty at times of such misdemeanors, and music educators even more, with their peculiar gift of associating music with boredom and pedagogic nonsense.

But if you want to go into politics, you do best to study law; if you want to go into academic music, you do best to study musicology. Lawyers are no better fitted to govern than members of a dozen other professions, but theirs is the accepted avenue into government. The academic world has never felt easy with any musical calling until the musicologists came along. They speak the language of the learned, and they usually join their non-musical colleagues in the belief that the noisier aspects of music, like performance and practice, should be subdued. On the whole, a little of this erudition won't hurt you, but don't go the whole hog. Never let it get the upper hand. That is turning art inside out. "Schoolwork," said Gide, "consists of taming the classics; they appear tempered, softened, inoffensive; familiarity has dulled their sharpest weapons."

Concerning your larger aims, remember that your public is *the public*, not the professionals, and least of all, the other composers. Quite possibly the greatest music is that which reaches all levels.

Student: Could you name a few examples of what you have in mind?

Teacher: Well, *The Messiah, The St. Matthew Passion*, Gluck's *Orpheus, The Beggar's Opera, Don Giovanni*, the *Sonata Appassionata*, the *Unfinished Symphony*, Chopin's *G Minor Ballad*, the *Italian Symphony, Aida, Boris Godunov*, the *Tristan Prelude, Carmen*, the *Symphonie Pathétique*. Who goes away from these disappointed? It is your knowers of music you turn to for your skills. But it is the lovers of music, the amateurs, you *give yourself* to. "I look to the provincial and the amateur," said London's sharpest critic, "for honesty and genuine fecundity in art." It was Bernard Shaw.

Accent on Youth

The most unpolitic act an American musician can commit is to allow the passage of years. Along with our highly competitive concept of the art, we have ordained a well-nigh inexorable time-table for the recognition and arrival of talent. Nearly all our prizes and fellowships are circumscribed by age. Appointments and retirements follow the same pattern. The long unhurried growth required by some of the world's most mature artists is a process little understood in an environment where business expects speedy returns, and where even education veers this way and that with each new Sputnik. It is common knowledge that Milton, Titian, Hokusai, Franck, Verdi, Handel, Monet, Shaw, Gide, Michelangelo and Goethe arrived at their peak late in life, but the knowledge does not mix with our mores. We substitute energy for maturity. While our pioneering has about reached its geographic limits, its spirit is still everywhere in evidence. Along with reckless hope, we affect a reckless disregard for the exhaustibility of resources which, in the arts, are the lives and spirits of men and women.

Thus *we believe less in achievement than in promise.* If an artist denies society the early discovery of his promise, society will deny him then his later fulfillment. It is willing and eager

112

to acclaim a young man on the slightest provocation. If then he withdraws himself, the better to merit this early praise—which may easily, as the Japanese say, "become the beginning of blame" —and to develop himself quietly for greater things, he soon loses touch with that potent genie of "recognition"; and then one day when he is ready to reappear with something salient, he finds that no effort will recover his rightful place. In the end he probably will be forced into the ranks of posthumity, which in the American arts are very impressive. (Poe, Melville, Thoreau, Dickinson, Ryder, MacDowell, and Ives are but the most notable examples.)

"Alas for America," wrote Emerson, "the ungirt, the diffuse, profuse, procumbent . . . eager, solicitous, hungry, rabid, busy-bodied America, attempting many things, vainly ambitious to feel thy own existence and convince others of thy talents, by attempting and hastily accomplishing much; yes, catch thy breath; fever and speed are never greatness; but reliance and serenity and waiting."

Ours is a bandwagon psychology in which an artist is driven to advertise himself before there is anything worth advertising. If he waits until his fruit is ripe, he waits already too long. "Who shall tell all the thoughts and feelings of Pierre in that desolate and shivering room," writes Melville, "when at last he knew that the wiser and profounder he should grow, the more he lessened his chances for bread."

The musical arts have their varied calendar of maturity. The dancer and the instrumentalist, beginning their training in early childhood, arrive the first, often in early youth. The singer is physiologically compelled to await maturity, and begins to be at his brief best seldom before his thirties. The composer, whose technical schooling is far more complex, including usually an instrumental mastery, must ordinarily pass through his imitative years, and is unlikely to arrive at a personal style and mastery before his late thirties. The conductor, whose training, apart from highly involved technicalities, requires long experience with the literature, and who must acquire social and pedagogic graces as well in order that his authority be accepted, is seldom at his best before forty, and thereafter continues to develop his art into old age. The critic, who should have weathered the temptation to elevate himself by depressing others, and who should have seen and heard vast amounts of works and performances, should rarely be given the power to make public appraisals before arriving in his mellower years. These are wide generalizations, allowing for many exceptions.

The calendar of decline corresponds, roughly. Dancing and singing are the first to give out; then instrumental playing; and lastly conducting and composing. The conductors who achieved their peak of mastery in late life include: Toscanini, Walter, Monteux, Stokowski, Koussevitsky, Scherchen, Ansermet, Reiner, Mitropoulos, Munch, and Stock. Few young men could compete with this group. Thus it is that the American system of prizes, which usually excludes any contestant over thirty-five, has virtue (and then only limited) for the instrumentalist and singer alone, but none whatever for the composer and the conductor, who are, in America even more than abroad, often just getting into their stride at that age. There is an odd and self-defeating disparity between the premium we place on American youth on the one hand, and on European maturity on the other. If we engage an American conductor, we specify he must be "young." But we search abroad for men in their ripest years. The afore-mentioned conductors all came to America in middle age. And it is precisely here in America that the native conductor, with practically no opera houses, and scarcely a look into the assistant positions in the orchestra, requires more time to prepare himself than anywhere else.

With the teacher it is the same. He grows with the years. Yet nearly all universities retire their professors at sixty-five, possibly on a premise borrowed from industry, which requires competitive energy and performing efficiency of its employees. In certain fields, such as salesmanship and business, competition never stops. But in teaching, while there is doubtless a competitive spirit among the younger men and women in their search for security and personal advancement, there is no reason to continue this on the higher levels, once rank and tenure are secure. The self-perfection that follows on competition as the teacher matures avails the salesman or industrialist little, but it rounds out the teacher. This is the age of tolerance and understanding, when ambition and self-seeking have worn off. If a man is a dullard then, he is sure to have been one at twenty-five as well.

Recollecting my own college years, it was the older men I remember the most warmly as teachers and advisers. As a rule, the younger men seemed insecure in their presentation and organization of subject matter. The art of lecturing (and who will deny that it is an art?) requires long time and experience to acquire. It is the same with the art of conducting discussion. With due allowance for the rapid changes in medicine and the physical sciences, where younger men are more attuned to the newer developments, one must not overlook that the bulk of the liberal and fine arts courses deal primarily with subjects whose weight lies in the past, and this is certainly true in music.

An age of de-individualization, like the present, likes nothing better than to plan every man's curriculum of life, from grade school up. Whatever statistical attractions this may have, it is the artist who fits the least well into such patterns. He is the traditional bulwark of individualism, and is its last champion. The flowering of artistic personality is not to be predicted. A Pergolesi, a Mozart, a Purcell, a Schubert, a Raphael, a Keats: these men have completed a life work before a Wagner, a Verdi, a Franck, a Milton, or a Hokusai have barely gotten started. Let us not legislate on these matters, in favor of youth or age, either one.

What should count is not the age of a contestant or candidate, but his vitality and stature. A Titian painting masterpieces at ninety is as much a prodigy as a Mozart writing operas at nine. As yet no one has invented a yardstick by which an artist may be "evaluated" by his age in years. Besides, it is better to engage a master even at the beginning of his decline than a mediocrity on the rise. Mount Blanc on the far side is still Mount Blanc, and the molehill over there is still a molehill. *"Ehret eure Meister*—honor your masters," said Wagner through the lips of Sachs. Every horse is made to work till his strength gives out. But the intellectual man is put out to pasture because some clerk has kept his eye on the calendar.

*The American imitations of Europe will always
lack interest and vitality, as all derivations do.*
ALFRED NORTH WHITEHEAD

The Search

Though the world seldom asks today for deep and sustained thought, we have still the anomaly of the long symphony. It is a brave gesture in this day of explosives; when permanent buildings seem the least safe; when eggs are scattered in many baskets. The painter gives us mostly only a sketch or a doodle. The day of great canvases is over, and even the muralists Orozco and Rivera have left us. But the full-dress symphony goes on like the obsolete battleship, with all its minutiae of scoring, its complexity, its laboriousness in creation, its expensiveness in preparation and performance. The time has come to recognize smaller works once more, not necessarily to the detriment of the large. It is only that largeness has so usurped the field that there are neither honors nor rewards for the writer on a modest scale. Are brevity and economy then a fault?

"Rather than the ponderous permanent blunders," said Frank Lloyd Wright, "until we learn more of good appropriate building, why not ephemera as preliminary studies, say?"

Consider only what a role the smaller writings have played in literature. Without them a host of great names would disappear: Donne, Herrick, Burns, Heine, Poe, Mörike, Housman, Dickinson. Or the lyric painters: Chardin, Blake, Cezanne, Van

117

Gogh, Whistler, Ryder. Or the lyric music makers: Domenico
Scarlatti, Chopin, Wolf, Grieg, Fauré, Debussy.

"Why is a symphony better," asked Chopin; "just because it
is bigger?" Even some of the mightiest of symphonists were able
in the course of brief works to create some of their greatest
statements, as for example, the *Fantasy in C Minor* for piano of
Mozart, the *Coriolanus Overture* of Beethoven, the *Erlking* of
Schubert, and certain *Etudes* of Chopin. The *Gettysburg Address*,
briefest of all orations, outlives all the speeches of the New World,
yet was received in its day as a "flat failure. . . . Mr. Lincoln
did most foully traduce the motives of the men who were slain."
His critics thought the heroes deserved many words, a symphonic
speech such as Everett gave them. Today our patrons and the
musical public still believe they deserve many notes of music.

It is quite possible and even likely, that the best of contemporary American music will ultimately prove to have been cast
in small forms. Perhaps, as Virgil Thomson has pointed out,
"the ideal of the 'masterpiece' has led us astray in an era not
fitted for its inception, despite the large orchestra which remains
to satisfy our need for an older literature, and whose existence
explains the continued attempts to create great symphonies."
The anomaly is that the orchestra, the very vehicle for ample and
expanded musical eloquence, remains the most inaccessible of
all media to the American writers of today; yet it continues to
arrogate our main attention and support.

While many an American was combing the researches of
postwar European theorists and innovators in the Twenties,
Thirties, and early Forties in the hope of finding some new
acorn to plant in his native soil, he overlooked a native seed
which, by virtue of historical parallel, should have promised the
most bountiful growth of all, namely, the use of his own language.
To the native musical writer of today, poetry, English and
American, could be the simplest and most reliable guide to an
indigenous style. Its meters and its subject matter would decide
the geometry of melody, its curves and cadences, its pace and
the cast of its forms. Here is an inexhaustible living resource,

and its appropriate use must inevitably restore music to its pristine singability again, however different that may be from its Italian, French, or German prototypes. The processes of speech (the breath, the inflections, the accent, the nuances, the characters, the length of syllables, the phrasings) how could these help but guide him into a music that had the unmistakable imprint of American thought?

Once we give our music this nativity, paradoxically we give it wings with which it will fly all over the world. Nothing is more provincial than the current attempt to be international in art. Every region of the world has its special foods which the whole world enjoys: potatoes in Idaho, coffee in Brazil, wine in France, and pineapples in the Philippines. The taste for these, as for music, is a sort of universal tongue, but the origins are localized, and the more so the wider the product's appeal. We are looking all the time for an indigenous American music. We have it in jazz. When Europe heard *Porgy and Bess* it sighed and said, "At last, a real American work"—all this after hearing ever so many symphonies sponsored by our well-disposed State Department in its cultural programs abroad. But of most of these symphonies Europeans had been saying, "This is all very good, but it is *our* music, all over again, transplanted perhaps, considerably de-sexed, but nothing more. It gives us no feeling of a new world."

I am not promoting jazz. It needs no promotion. The world is waiting for some serious great American works.

You can't write fifty songs to Whitman and still sound like a Frenchman. You can't do a cycle of Emily Dickinson in the manner of Hugo Wolf. You can't do an opera on O'Neill in the manner of Strauss. And the Schönberg style will avail you nothing when you tackle Sandburg, or Melville, or Frost, or Jeffers.

What these poets need, if indeed anything at all, is a new kind of music; and the miracle is that the new will present itself unbidden without aid of new theories or a new esthetic. That is not to say that the poems need melodies at all, but perhaps the melodies need the poems to activate them. "In one branch of our art," says Vaughan Williams, "it is hardly possible for an artist to be untrue to himself, namely, when he writes for the human voice, for then language takes command and the natural rise and fall of the words must suggest the melodic and rhythmic outline."

Language may well be the greatest single factor in new and original music. Every time artists turned toward their own literature, whether it was Luther, or Schütz, or Purcell, or Rameau, or Mozart, or Glinka, or Chopin, or Moussorgsky, or Smetana, or Sullivan, or Vaughn Williams, or Ives, or De Falla, or Villa-Lobos, or Bartok, the result was new music. No instrument, no theory, nothing can surpass language, as a catalytic agent not only to precipitate new music, but to fasten its nativity, and with that, paradoxically and in course of time, its universality.

I have spoken elsewhere about the preponderance of instrumentalism today. The instrument can do anything, play any succession of notes you will, skip any intervals, deviate from any tonality, and surpass any vocal range, all without effort. The temptation to write melodies along such purely instrumental lines is evidence of our desire to create something new. The question is, are these indeed melodies, when they are not conceivable in the human larynx? It is true that melodies have long transcended any single vocal range, but that does not mean they were not vocally conceived. We could say Bach was more instrumentally inclined than Handel, Beethoven more than Mozart, Chopin more than Mendelssohn, but the fact remains that these all started out from a vocal basis, and they all wrote for the voice, even Chopin; his early songs are a prototype of his later mazurkas. Only in our day have there been composers who did not see fit to write any vocal music; and some are turning to it in their later careers.

The voice will not be denied. It is nature in music.

Along with the other arts music has tended toward abstraction, but in a different way, for it is less representational and more nearly "abstract" to begin with. The abstractional trend is less clearly delimited. (Wishing to discover similarities between the arts, we must not lose sight of differences.) There seems to be some strengthening through abstracting the elements in every art; but what happens after the threshold of complete abstraction is crossed is not clear. The art has then traveled the entire road from the "idea-less" thing to the "thing-less" idea. Is this latter extreme a tenable resting point any more than its opposite, particularly for an art that is not primarily decorative? Unmattered idea may be as incomplete as unspirited matter. The danger is that out-and-out abstraction may have shed its humanity.

To discover and realize the vertebrate quality of steel in a tower is right, but the tower is the end, and not the steel. The arts have those felicitous moments when design and object have become one, but they are the exceptions, often the accidents. Nevertheless, we are so impressed by them that we tend to invest the arts more and more with the condition of this same fulfillment, with the result that we exalt design, abstraction and formulation at the cost of whatever in our thinking and feeling is organic, anthropoid, sympathetic, representative, social, and tangible. It is the triumph of physics over physiology. Seeking to transcend matter, we become materialist.

The painter paints "pure" geometry, the composer polyphonates "pure" melodic line, each thinking thereby to touch upon the subconscious of the hearer or listener and to reveal sympathetically thereby something of his own subconscious. The error is to believe that the intangible is conveyed through the intangible.

Shadow gives no shadow. There is a danger, too, in attempting to reveal the ultimate secrets of the personality. One may encounter at last only a void. It is like walking through the door of a movie prop and finding nothing behind. Probably the true realm of purely abstract art, whether in painting, music, or letters, is the decorative. Here the abstraction serves something outside itself; and thus does not carry the main burden, as indeed it cannot.

Words being the most specific and commonplace of our artistic media, literature has been most nearly spared the dangers of abstraction, and has proven itself the most characteristic, fruitful, and powerful form of present-day art. This, alone, should give pause to painters and writers of music, in their present speculations.

Within one generation, I have seen America redefined from the pioneer land that had not yet had time for its arts, and "possessed no folk music" on which to build, to the land that is but an extension of Europe on a new soil, and is literally wallowing in its folk music. Meanwhile it has not only absorbed all of Europe's music, but also its esthetic politics. Every new doctrine from abroad is avidly seized upon here—much more so than over there—as if we too were caught in the same artistic cul-de-sac, and were scrambling to get out. The question is whether these doctrines have any real validity with us, or whether their popularity here is only a mark of imitativeness. For they seem to be largely the flowers of ennui. What place have they in a fecund soil like ours? We shared in Europe's last wars, but not to the extent of sharing in their full aftermath of destruction and despair. Is it profitable for us to take so to heart these artistic gestures of desolation? "Now all the artists are afraid of nature," says Mestrovic. Are the highest flights of our language to be word puzzles? Is the face of nature and of man to be exalted in a doodle? Does Orpheus know no better place to lead us than into a physics laboratory?

The problem is older than we like to imagine. In Weimar nearly one and one-half centuries ago, Goethe remarked to Eckermann: "All eras in a state of decline and dissolution are subjective; on the other hand, all progressive eras have an objective tendency. Every healthy effort is directed from the inward to the outward world, as you see in all great eras which were really in a state of progression, and all of an objective nature."

Another change is taking place, more quietly, and has not yet attracted attention. While we speak ever more of rhythm in music, is rhythm not slipping quietly out of our everyday lives? The horse's trot has yielded to the purr of the motor. Walking is confined to the New York pavements where cars have no longer any room to move. Our footfall is supplanted by the whine of rubber. The plow horse's plodding step has become the rattle of the tractor. The churning of butter, the scrubbing of clothes, the sweeping of floors: all these have been made obsolete by machines. The pickaxe is seen no more on our pavements, and the hammer is yielding to a pneumatic gun. Hay is pitched and barrels are propelled, bales and boxes are hoisted —all today without the rhythms and swaying of the body and the accompanying songs of yesterday. The systole and diastole of the steam engine give way now to the drum-fire of the diesel. The canoe, once moved with long body strokes, is now pushed *martellato* by an outboard. Wheels are everywhere supplanting our legs, arms, and fingers.

The present ideal of perfect smoothness, and of streamlining, must somehow touch the arts no less than our persons. The pulsations of the older music may eventually have no counterpart in our daily lives. Perhaps the inordinate vogue of jazz, and its various offspring, is to be explained as compensatory to the disappearance of physical rhythm because of the machines.

MUSIC AND SOCIETY

Have I not as good a title to laugh as men have to be ridiculous, and to expose vice as another has to be vicious?

J. SWIFT

Are Musicians Citizens?

Whatever one may say about nationalism, or "nativism," as Whitman called it, will—however ample the qualifications one may make—arouse controversy. No musician is indifferent to any possible shift of balance affecting his prestige, his employment, or his market. There are large vested interests in music and of these none is more pronounced than a certain anationalism that accompanies the snob appeal of the artist from foreign parts, and our concomitant inferiority complex. One is hesitant to open up so touchy a subject not only because of the misunderstandings that are bound to result, but even more because of the danger one envisages in the prospect of a reversal of the present situation, once the scales are tipped. One does not wish to participate in a revolution of which it may later be said, to paraphrase Emerson: One wonders if the revolt was worth the trees shot down.

America is Europe's cultural child. Having now grown up, it poses the ancient problems of youth as against age, of ambition, freedom, and secession, as against experience, fidelity and authority. The foremost Americans in music have mostly studied with Europeans, both here and abroad, and among them few, if any, have not retained grateful memories of Paris, Vienna,

127

Rome, London, or Berlin, not only for the instruction and hospitality they experienced there, but for the attitude they encountered toward the art, which was one of deep respect, and even reverence. Today the American has little more to learn from Europe in technique or factual knowledge. But he has a great deal to learn about the labor and dedication that an art requires, and the rich rewards this will yield. He is bound to be pleasantly surprised at first at the esteem in which the artist is held in many circles abroad, and is equally shocked on returning home to discover that he is judged not by his art, but by the degree of success it has yielded him.

Americans who have been abroad a year or more find it difficult to acclimatize themselves at home on their return, and many would be ready to beat a retreat to Europe, if they could find employment there. But Europe protects its artists against anything but sporadic invasions from the New World; and the American is forced to find his berth at home, which ought to be the best thing in the world for him. Only a few American opera singers have of late made their permanent home abroad, preferring a subsistence wage with a genuine artistic and professional activity over there, along with great popularity, to a more comfortable income with all the career substitutes—such as teaching, church singing, radio entertainment, night clubs, music clubs—over here; a clear case where fidelity to art and country do not coincide. It should be added that these singers are not, like some of our writers, expatriates by choice, but rather by necessity.

The returning American who must make a living in what at first seems to him artistically a veritable circus-land, should eventually discover some real rewards at home. These rewards are seldom obvious in his own particular calling, and may best be learned of in our literature, the most domesticated of the arts. They are found not in the well-advertised physical comforts, but in a hidden undercurrent of buoyancy and optimism (quite the opposite of the Chamber of Commerce sort): a faith in new vitality and genius, a faith in the *worthwhileness* and the future of creative art, that is already fairly spent overseas, despite the greater institutional activity; a faith in *the ultimate artistic triumph of democracy* (not to be confused with the democratic triumph in art) despite its corruptions and vulgarizations. An enduring solace awaits him on the banks of that steady brown stream of native thought, that carried Jefferson and Lincoln, Emerson and Whitman, Lanier and Whittier, Winslow Homer and Henri, Mark Twain and Henry James, MacDowell and Ives, and is flowing strongly today, even though lost in the dismal swamp of a progress-weary society.

He learns to accept America as a permanent anomaly. It wise-cracks at Heaven, and is pious over Hell. But if a man goes beneath the surface, he will dig up all the hope and enterprise he needs to make him walk upright, despite indifference and neglect. In Vienna, they ask you wistfully why you should be writing music at all today, when Schubert lived just around the corner, and Beethoven wrote his *Eroica* on the fringe of town. But for the American, Whitman is still loitering on the Capitol steps, telling a Senate clerk, "All is eligible to all, all is for you."

Why, then, bring up the delicate, uneasy theme of nationalism? Because it is important for a nation to *realize itself* at the right time and not go on forever dreaming of its future. We are today the future of a past that dreamt highly of us. In many affairs, our "future" is already past, and I do not care to see music settle down to a pedestrian mediocrity at the very moment it should spread its wings and fly. If a nation neglects its music, it can doubtless be great in other things. But we do not neglect music; we only neglect our musicians. We refuse to recognize that they have become mature and are ready to assume major responsibilities. We ask them to go on learning, when further learning can only blunt their morale, inhibit too long their aspiration to achieve.

What do we mean by nationalism in music? Is it a thing of citizenship? Are we asking for laws? Are we talking of exclusion? At the risk of censure for extracting remarks out of their context, I give a few brief opinions on nationalism.

Einstein is quoted as saying: "Nationalism is an infantile disease. It is the measles of mankind."

Oscar Wilde said: "Art is the science of beauty, and mathematics the science of truth; there is no national school of either. Indeed, a national school is a provincial school nearly."

Goethe speaks of a degree: "Where a person stands to a certain extent above nations, and feels the weal or woe of a neighboring people as if it had happened to his own."

In another vein, Ibsen said: "Culture is unthinkable apart from national life."

Walt Whitman reiterates this theme in most of his writings: "Underneath all, nativity . . . men, women, cities, nations are only beautiful from nativity."

And from Melville: "While fully acknowledging all excellence everywhere, we should refrain from unduly lauding foreign writers, and at the same time, duly recognize the meritorious writers that are our own, those writers who breathe that unshackled, democratic spirit of Christianity in all things, which now takes the practical lead in this world, though at the same time led by ourselves—us Americans."

Then there are opinions that qualify.

Daniel Gregory Mason says: "Nationalism is excellent as an ingredient, but disastrous as a dogma."

Van Wyck Brooks: "Too much nationalism is as bad as too little."

Clearly the term is differently used. Einstein and Goethe are speaking of a nationalism that measures love, hate or indifference of one people toward another according to the political temperature.

Wilde is speaking of an insularity that measures native art by other standards than foreign art, that groups artists by geography rather than by talent or accomplishment.

Ibsen is merely saying that an art, like a plant, must have roots in a suitable soil, and cannot be replanted indiscriminately.

Whitman stresses nativity, but allows for this everywhere. His is a universal theme of nationality.

Melville is defending the American writer against the snobbery of his time, which excluded most of his contemporaries from the literary sun.

Mason and Brooks say in effect that while the artistic plant grows best in native soil, the circumstance is nothing to boast of.

What then is our present theme of nationalism? Would American artists advocate something akin to a protective tariff in order to be spared the competition of foreigners? There are many that would, and their argument would be simply one of *reciprocity,* for European nations have long excluded the American musician by stronger devices than a tax. They seldom allow him to make a living without taking out citizenship, and that requires years of residence, which presupposes means and enforces professional idleness in the interim. Thus there has never been a fair exchange between us who have wealth in excess and the Europeans who, with their wealth of institutions, have opportunity in abundance. Only in Germany and Austria can singers today find opportunity, provided in most cases they are supported from the United States. A few singing careers have been launched in Italy, but not with Italian support. The career possibilities of American conductors abroad are nil.

Nearly all our industries were built up with the aid of tariffs, and are dependent on their continuance. The first World War taught us the need for a native chemical industry, independent of Germany. We learned the technique and then protected ourselves with tariffs, and within one generation assumed the lead. But in music we impose tariffs not on foreigners, but on ourselves. It is the American who must pay great sums to management to be allowed a place at the domestic dinner table, the very while he is still helping to support Europe's musical temples (foreign aid has gone into music as well as the military), and inviting its priests here to take over his own.

The present situation in America is described with good analogy in a letter of Sir Arthur Sullivan's, written before the turn of the century. It reads:

"There is a deal of nonsense talked about no nationality in art.

That is very well but there *is* nationality in the artist. . . . What is the use of founding scholarships and educating hundreds of young people, if you shut all the doors against them when they are ready to enter the world by choosing the foreigner for everything? The result of it all is that at the present moment, our schools of music are turning out highly trained paupers. . . . Everyone must have noticed that foreign conductors are accepted here with open arms. English conductors are comparatively few in number, but when the foreign conductor returns to his own country, taking English money away with him, you will find that he never reciprocates by performing an English composer's music. . . . I have never had the smallest help or encouragement (in behalf of English musicians) from the press, or even the musicians themselves. The latter are listless, indifferent; the former either absolutely neutral, or actively favorable to the foreigner."

A glance at the repertory of any of America's orchestras will confirm the parallel with Sullivan's England. American works and performers, while they are more in evidence today than a generation ago, are still the stepchildren, and their selection shows little initiative or independence. Always the same few safe names! Of America's major orchestras, of which there are anywhere between twenty and thirty, depending on the yardstick, less than a fourth or fifth are in native hands; of the operas, none are. I cannot say the Americans would be more deserving of these posts. I only say they have not been permitted to compete fairly save where management has consented, and that implies financial transactions that most Americans can neither afford nor condone. Management has always favored the European, except when forced to do otherwise.

The interesting sequel to Sullivan's criticism is that England has since his day largely nationalized its music, and has thereby raised itself to a leading place in the modern musical world. This was not accomplished, however, by the "listless and indifferent" musicians Sullivan describes, but rather by the energetic and purposeful efforts of men of the stamp of Edward Elgar, Vaughn Williams, Cecil Forsythe, Henry Wood, Thomas Beecham, and

Malcolm Sargent. They realized, as we must soon realize, that the English composer could never come into his own without all English music coming into its own as well, meaning the performers, the writers, the singers, the conductors, and the stage directors. England is cordial to artists from the world over, but quite definitely favors its own for the posts of large responsibility.

Quoting from Vaughn Williams: "Whistler used to say that it was as ridiculous to talk about national art as of national chemistry. In saying this, he failed to see the difference between art and science. Science is the pure pursuit of knowledge and thus knows no boundaries. Art, and especially the art of music, uses knowledge as a means to the evocation of personal experience in terms that will be intelligible to and command the sympathy of others."

In 1911, Cecil Forsythe wrote: "We must begin to realize, as the French, the Germans, and the Italians have already realized, that all foreign art products come to a nation not only as the parents of possible new ideas, but also as the children of an organism that has been molded to its present complexity and perfection only after centuries of intellectual and emotional struggle. In this struggle, we have had almost no share, and it is therefore merely prudent (if nothing else) that we should examine its results narrowly in order to ascertain how much or how little can be of use to us. To do this, we must first rid ourselves of our national habit of musical acquiescence."

Will anyone say of Mozart that he was insular when he introduced his native language for the first time into German opera? Or that Glinka and the Russian Five did wrong in working to establish the propriety and necessity of a Russian music for Russians, against the snobbery of the aristocracy, who believed music spoke only in the French or the Italian tongue? Or that English musicians have not fully warranted the movement that had its first articulate expression with Sullivan, and that was described in its earlier stages, particularly by those continentals who saw their opportunities jeopardized, as evidence of a petty provincialism? "Who are you, indeed," said Walt Whitman, "who would talk or sing to America? Have you studied out the land, its idioms and men? Have you learned the physiology, politics, geography, pride, freedom, friendship of the land?"

Though we are younger in music than the English, the national theme is by no means new here. Already prior to the Civil War, William Fry wrote: "It is very bad taste, to say the least, for men to bite the hand that feeds them. While America has thus far been able to do the chief things for the dignity of man, forsooth she must be denied the brains for original art, and must stand like a beggar, cap in hand. . . . It is the duty of the musician not alone to criticize the errors which may be committed in his adopted country, but also *to tender his unqualified support* in word and deed, to the end that such errors may be rectified."

Our own recent situation has been well described by Albert Goldberg in the *Los Angeles Times* when he said: "In a nation dedicated to freedom of opportunity for all, the American musician, alone in the entire professional field and practically alone among workers in the other arts, has consistently been denied by his fellow countrymen the general recognition which would permit him to attain and hold the majority of the top flight positions in his profession. Americans respect, admire and patronize their own doctors, lawyers, engineers, and scientists. They offer no particular hindrance to the progress of American writers, painters and sculptors. But by and large they accept musicians of their own kind only under special and exceptional circumstances, and never in any period of their history have they fortified the native musician, except in the trade union commercial market, against the encroachment and competition of the foreign musician.

"The American concert industry, in effect an international cartel, welcomes and exploits them [European talents]; its profit and loss philosophy involves no patriotic conscience and no responsibility to the American musician. There have been several conducting positions open among major American orchestras and Europeans have been elected to fill all of them, in most cases without giving any American a chance to demonstrate his abilities.

"When orchestras wish to vary the routine of a permanent conductor with guest conductors, it is visiting Europeans who are invited, and the new music they present is not by American composers but by nationals of their own country. But of proven American musical talent in all lines, there is a plentiful supply and it is all going to wither on the vine unless someone does a bit of flag-waving—and quickly."

Excluded here, then, because he *is not* a foreigner, and abroad because he *is* a foreigner, the American musician remains musically a man without a country.

Patrons

Patronage has always been needed. Artists are sometimes, though
rarely, wealthy. Occasionally, one of them breaks through the
barriers of apathy or prejudice and achieves success and wealth.
The error consists in mistaking this exception for the rule. The
arts can no more subsist on their own than can the schools. This
has been wholly misunderstood in American government circles,
where recognition of the arts happened only once in the nation's
history, and then only to alleviate the destitution into which they,
along with other professions, had fallen. Men whose works have
posthumously reaped countless millions for publishers, galleries,
collectors, and more recently radio and record companies, have
had to live in their day from hand to mouth, and have even starved
or died from neglect.

We are doing no worse by the artist in the twentieth century
in the matter of his living, but let us not delude ourselves into
thinking we are doing much better. A Mozart or a Schubert need
no longer languish in beggary today, for either could probably
find employment in some American school—provided he had the
required "education credits," a matter largely of a few fees and
the patience to suffer a prescribed period of academic boredom.
Perhaps the main difference between Europe and America lies

in that the former often starved its artists in the belly, while the latter mostly starves them in the soul—it looks better. It would be interesting to add up the fortunes that have been made on Mozart' and Schubert since their death. I wonder if Lloyd's of London might not conceivably handle some sort of posterity insurance for artists. If it were to yield only the tiniest percentage of ultimate returns, men such as these could live in comfort if not affluence. Of course there is a school that believes artists must suffer in order to be good artists. Certain it is that the community of suffering will not admit anyone into its secrets who has not himself suffered. But the world's sources of misery seem bountiful enough today without adding starvation and contempt, which are the more conspicuous when framed by the vast superfluities we flaunt now before the world. Affluence did not undermine the artistic integrity of Verdi, Handel, Mendelssohn, Brahms, Puccini, Turner, Manet, Cezanne, Winslow Homer, Shaw, Byron, Flaubert, Gide or Goethe all of whom did enjoy or achieve security and recognition.

It is not that an artist requires wealth or even prosperity. He is usually indifferent to money until its absence becomes a predicament, for then he must spend more of his energies on resolving his debts than he would otherwise spend on acquiring a surplus. Luxury may be pleasant to experience on occasion, but it is not for him to live with. It cuts him off, not only from his fellow artists, but from the world at large, which he will never fully understand from the sheltered vantage point of wealth and privilege. There have been great artists with large means, but the means mostly came unbidden, or else were built up as a bulwark of protection against the hostile fate to which the world has ever condemned what it will later love the most. One of the affluent, Goethe, says: "In a splendid abode, I am instantly lazy and inactive. Contrarily a small residence like this poor apartment, where a sort of disorderly order prevails, suits me exactly. It allows my nature full liberty to act, and to create from itself alone."

American philanthropy always starts with the temples. What

is to fill them is secondary. They become a shell into which the living thing must then fit itself. How much better if the two grew together. You cannot be at ease in such a place; the expectations it awakens dog you at every step. What a day it will be when we once learn to build our foundations for culture on the man, rather than his mansion.[1]

But the real poverty of the artist—shall we absolve society from all responsibility for this merely because there be those who have triumphed not over it but despite it? Are we absolved from a former generation's indifference merely because we put a tremendous price today on the works their authors could not even sell?

"I am not indifferent to money," wrote Van Gogh, "but I do not understand the wolves. . . . If for a moment I feel rising within me the desire for a life without care, for prosperity, each time I go fondly back to the trouble and the cares, to a life full of hardship, and think it is better so, I learn more from it, and make progress. This is not the road on which one perishes. *If only the trouble and the cares do not become unbearable.* . . . In order to be a link in the chain of artists, we are paying a high price, in health, in youth, in liberty, none of which we have any joy of."

The old patron *liked* art rather than *used* it. Sometimes he loved it. Very often he was himself a cultivated amateur artist, and had abilities that were well-nigh professional. Kings composed music; princes painted pictures; and none were ashamed of a life of poetry. Patron and artist were quite often friends and worked together; the one proposing, the other executing. Supply and demand, talent and taste, went together. It was then the Doge of Venice instead of yesterday's W.P.A.; the Medici rather than Firestone Rubber; Esterhazy rather than the Petrillo Fund;

---

[1] By virtue of Mme. von Meck's stipends to Tschaikovsky, which totaled less than the amount to endow one fellowship today, Russia had the honor of producing what I believe to be the greatest symphonist since Beethoven (yes, I have not forgotten the noble Brahms). She was actuated by her feeling that his music was beautiful. In her benefactions, she consulted with no experts nor engaged any intermediary; nor did she "endow in perpetuity."

the Archduke Rudolf instead of U.S. Steel; Mme. von Meck rather than the Federated Music Clubs. The patron did not commission Titian, Michelangelo, Haydn, Beethoven, or Tschaikovsky for primarily civic or altruistic reasons. He did so because he wanted to possess, or have the honor to bring to light, works of lasting worth and beauty. It was a public service privately achieved. The possession mattered little beside the result, a masterpiece.

By contrast, the American patron, whose largesse exceeds in amount that of all the patrons of the past, has seldom seen the need to prepare himself for the responsibility of giving. "Almost any man," said Thoreau, "knows how to earn money, but not one in a million knows how to spend it." He knows too little about art, and he is afraid of his own reactions to it. He has a mortal fear of being "taken in." As a result, he wraps his benevolence up in the most impersonal philanthropies. A building, a foundation, a school, an institution with an untouchable capital sum, all these seem to guarantee permanence and incorruptibility. Living by, and working with large corporations, he puts his faith in a corporation whose business it is to dispense rather than acquire money. It goes with the common saying that "the institution is greater than the individual," a belief promulgated mainly and paradoxically in this land founded on liberty and individualism. The sum of men is conceived to be better than the man.

But he forgets that taxes, upkeep, and the weather can reduce a building in less than a lifetime. Inflation, politics and self-seeking may destroy anything. Administration can become a parasite that eats up finally more than it disburses. It is as hard to find the man to administer with tact and perspicacity such large monies and institutions as it is to find the artist worthy of their subvention. Wherever there is too much money, barnacles grow thick; and the philanthropic ship often finds itself resting on the sands of some lazy lagoon, a hazard and an obstruction to normal traffic.

In illustrating the various features of American patronage, the grander aspects are exemplified in bequests such as those of

Mr. Henry Lee Higginson of Boston, Mr. William Andrews Clark of Los Angeles, and Mr. Henry H. Reichold of Detroit to symphony orchestras; Mr. George Eastman of Rochester and Mrs. Curtis Bok of Philadelphia to schools; Mrs. Edith Rockefeller McCormick of Chicago and Mr. Otto Kahn of New York to operas, to name but a few. They undertook to do privately what was, and still is, done by the state or the municipality abroad. Figured in terms of creative music, what one of these patrons has given to the art would probably aggregate a sum sufficient to have subsidized all the great composers of the last three or four centuries, with enough left over to pay for the publication of all their works.

Yet, few masterpieces, if any, of the first water, have resulted directly from these gigantic gifts, although they have given us the greater part of our musical higher education and entertainment, and therefore deserve the public's gratitude. They laid a foundation ample enough for the development of a great school of American conductors, soloists, and composers, had such an end been desired and fostered, and had the responsibility toward national art been realized. Surely three, four, and five generations should have sufficed to make us self-sufficient. As it is, our orchestras and operas remain largely dependent on leadership from abroad, as in the past. This is a type of patronage which with shrinking individual fortunes, and a growing population of artists, will ultimately have to be assumed by government, whether state, municipal, or national.

More effective toward the realization of an *indigenous creative art* has been the program of the Guggenheim Foundation, which has, for more than a generation, been granting fellowships to creative artists of all kinds, irrespective of rank or reputation, relieving them for a year or two at least, of the heavy routines imposed by teaching, commercial art or music, or whatever means of livelihood they have found it necessary to engage in, within a civilization which uses them chiefly in secondary capacities.

More recently, a number of universities and colleges have established teaching posts bearing titles such as: "composer-in-residence," "poet-in-residence," "artist-in-residence," in an attempt to lay emphasis on original work, and to bring students into contact with persons who do such work. It parallels the "research-professorship" in science. Among schools that have the distinction of having introduced this worthy practice should be mentioned: Harvard, Yale, Cornell, Syracuse, Michigan, Georgia, Indiana, and Illinois Universities, as well as Colorado, George Peabody, Bennington, Mills, and Mt. Holyoke Colleges. This list is by no means all-inclusive.

No brighter chapter in American patronage can be found than the MacDowell Colony. Conceived by the first of America's major musical figures, Edward MacDowell, and realized by his widow, through two generations of indefatigable labor and wise guidance this little New Hampshire farm with its two-dozen-odd studios scattered through woods and meadows has given poets, painters, composers, sculptors, and a few scholars an opportunity to work under conditions of undisturbed tranquility, and to enjoy the society and stimulation of their fellows. If the artistic products of this colony were to be removed from the gallery of American achievement, the gap would be formidable. More recently, Mr. Huntington Hartford has established a no less admirable colony near Los Angeles. Yaddo, at Saratoga, New York, and Montalvo at Saratoga, California, are smaller colonies actuated by similar worthy aims.

The very large foundations, such as Ford, Rockefeller, and Carnegie, have also begun to see the need to foster the creative arts. Much is to be hoped from their liberal commissioning plans. They are powerful and wealthy enough to accomplish for this country what governments have done abroad and what individual patrons can seldom now accomplish here, namely *activate institutions* so they may in turn become a proper home for all manner of talent.

Nevertheless, we must keep in mind that the responsibility of patronage grows with the sums involved. There is always a danger that in dealing with vast sums there can develop a certain contempt or indifference toward modest projects. How shall an artist formulate to the satisfaction of committees dealing in millions that he needs but a little sum to tide him over a piece of work, to enable him to make a record, or a small publication, or to have the parts of a symphonic work copied, or even to be relieved of accumulated small debts that bedevil him out of all the peace of mind needed to produce? Instead, the foundation is so anxious to avoid mistakes in its disbursements that it seals itself in policies, to satisfy which a man must invent subterfuges, pretend an interest in group matters and social programs that do not concern him, effectively conceal his direct and often desperate personal needs, and magnify his undertaking out of all proportion so as to make it seem impressive. The benefactor can become so entangled in cautions that he no longer sees what is really urgent. Quite probably the most pressing needs are the most modest. Already there has developed a new kind of career, that of the "grant-hopper," whereby a man or woman moves from one colony or grant to another, the while each success instructs him the better to improve his lot in the next one. It becomes a kind of chain-promotion process, sometimes legitimate, often wasteful.

Pampering art is not the way to help it. I am not for taking the struggle out of art; I am only against ignoring it or starving it. If the choice must be between hunger or surfeit, I think hunger is still the better of the two.

Let the foundations, who are only now learning the lessons of music patronage, keep in mind that it is the *creative individual* who must first be served. If they plan to help institutions, that is good, provided the institutions keep this in mind. The most mischievous of everyday axioms is "first come, first served." It puts a premium on white-collar beggary, and unsettles the man with serious preoccupations. For it is mostly true that while the superior man is at work, the inferior one is busy with his politics. Patronage entails taste and trust, and also courage. It takes a great deal of courage nowadays to act honestly according to your taste.

The Roosevelt Administration conceived The Works Progress Administration under Harry Hopkins with a far-reaching program for theatre, music, writing, and the plastic arts as a relief measure at a time of vast unemployment. The project was successful beyond expectation. Despite wasteful management, the inevitable dissensions, obstructions by local politicians, union attempts at exclusive control, the derision of opposing political parties, and the vicissitudes of having to steer clear of competition with private enterprise, not to forget the vigorous infiltration of Communism, W.P.A. was America's great day in the public arts. Its program and achievement deserve to be restudied today as a guide to future patronage of the arts by government.

There is yet another kind of patron, the most important of all, and the most unsung. It is the amateur, without whom all music-making would be vain. Whether it is with money or not, he supports music with his interest, love and understanding, and very often his active participation. To him, above all, the artist addresses his eloquence and looks for acknowledgment and criticism. Artist and amateur form a bond, like teacher and student.[2]

The Talmud says, "Yourself you must not separate from the public fate." Our artists need citizenship more than all the prizes,

[2] The amateur can be anything from a mere lover of music to an artist of stature. The novelist and historian, Paul Horgan, calls himself a "virtuoso-listener," and for years invited his friends and students to what he named the "Beethoven Society" in Roswell, New Mexico, at which regular programs with records, annotations, and discussions were held. The surgeon, Dr. Leo Eloesser, made his San Francisco apartment a home for chamber music through the leanest and most opulent years of the city's life, where amateurs and professionals met on the common ground of informal music-making, himself participating with his viola. Mr. Henry Drinker, the Philadelphia lawyer, leads an amateur choral society through formidable areas of the literature, with regular sessions in his home, supplementing this with a scholarly labor of the first importance, namely, the translation into admirable singable English of the entire choral works of Bach. Mr. Jacques Barzun has succeeded, through his biography of Berlioz, in bringing this hitherto neglected great French composer into our lives as perhaps no other person, writer or musician has done. We have memories of Mrs. Elizabeth Sprague Coolidge, chamber music's most munificent patron, who was a pianist in her own right. The definitive biography of Beethoven remains, after many years, that of Alexander Thayer, a consular official who devoted his life to the assembling of materials for this monumental work.

Here is but a partial picture of the amateur's diverse outlets, which are seen to be of significance measuring sometimes with the achievements of professionals. The Women's Music Clubs and Sororities are among America's great musical assets. Here again, professionals and amateurs meet on common ground.

foundations and fellowships. Only the existence of secure performing institutions can give them this. The composer is lost when writing in a vacuum. Only at his desk is he a monk, and then only in working out the problems conceived of in society. An ounce of performance is better than a pound of protection. One commission is worth ten layers of academic insulation. Security is not a substitute for success. Much of this bitterness in our modern music comes from frustration, and in time it evokes bitter reactions from the public. Not wanted, the artist soon makes himself unwantable. *Some love must be exchanged,* if music is to have lovable qualities. "I would like to see places in every neighborhood for good music by the best musicians," said the painter Robert Henri, "so that their precious influence might be spread over all the community. This, of course, could not be done so long as the only will comes from the box office."

The leadership of such an institution would plainly be a matter of paramount importance. Leadership is the crux of the whole matter. It is only greatness that discovers greatness. It is stature that permits stature, and accomplishment that invites accomplishment. It is also littleness that recognizes, and permits, only littleness. "No institution," said Emerson, "will be greater than the institutor." What is needed is a combination of artistic grandeur and creative imagination and, above all, generosity. A new theatre or opera would be doomed from the start were it dominated by an administration postulated on clerical punctilio and the usual business rule. What is never understood in our country is that business policies must be the servants of the arts. The artist may be wasteful and inefficient, but he is never so wasteful as the businessman when the latter insists on controlling matters of art of which he knows nothing. And it is this business element that has built the great citadel of centralization, which is universally believed in the profession to have acquired the full-blown structure of a "national duopoly," individual objection to which is professional suicide. Well, music is not the telephone system, nor the mails, nor steel. If it has taken on the corporative aspects of these enterprises, one cannot say it has risen to them, but only fallen.

Consider where artists have grown. Most of the writers of modern Ireland were associated at some time with the Abbey Theatre of Dublin. In our own South, some of the foremost writers wrote in their youth for the Playmakers Theatre at the University of North Carolina, one of the few collegiate institutions where the play has been superior to the textbook. Not the least of the dramatists of America learned their trade in the little theatres, Greenwich Village, Provincetown, and summer stock, and others. Germany's leading playwrights realized themselves through the little theatre in Weimar, which the local Duke entrusted, with uncommon perspicacity, to Goethe. Later, this same Weimar theatre, under the direction of Liszt, became the sounding board for Berlioz, Wagner, and many contemporaries. The Imperial (State) Opera House of Vienna under Mahler fostered some of the foremost operatic works of the near-present. These are the proper homes for adult education, as well as the cradles of masterpieces. Audiences and artists learn through the pleasurable and profitable interaction of give and take.

To understand now what we have as yet failed to achieve, compare the American theatre with the American symphony orchestra. One grew from the bottom up, the other from the top down. One lives mostly on modern fare, the other on the classics. One is indigenous, the other is largely alien. One is profitable, the other is costly. One invites authorship, the other repels it. One has made a new literature, while the other has discouraged it. Can there be any doubt which has produced more works of lasting value? How does patronage look in this picture?

One of the greatest mistakes is to believe that any patronage is better than none. "It all helps," we say with weary comfort, forgetting that the elevation to power of the inferior man means the robbing of opportunity for the superior man to compete fairly in the open market, however small it may be. One should be careful when interfering with the process whereby levels establish themselves normally through that immutable sense of worth that is to be found among all good craftsmen. The good carpenter is degraded when his work becomes subject to the direction and criticism of the bungler. To patronize the incompetent with the aid of undeserved subsidies is then to undo the competent. For, lacking his natural outlet of work, the ablest of men is robbed of his healthful relation to his society, which he might enjoy to at least some degree if there were no patronage whatever.

"To bring a mediocre man to success," said Delacroix, "might be called the Saturnalia of power. Power proves its strength to itself only by the strange abuse of crowning some absurdity with the palm of success, of insulting genius, the only strength that absolute power cannot attack. Caligula's giving the rank of commander to his horse, that imperial farce, has been played and will always be played a great number of times."

Whatever the shortcomings of private patronage to date, one must acknowledge its munificence and the altruism that motivated the greater part of it. Certain it is that it will not continue in the future on the scale of the past.

It is only reasonable that the agency that reduces present incomes and fortunes should assume part of the responsibility of fostering the arts henceforth. There remains no practical solution, but *governmental support of the arts,* and above all of music and drama. Every littlest principality abroad takes such support for granted. Our own government helps in fact to support Europe's state subsidies, for have we not been taxed to maintain the Marshall Plan? It is not unlikely that the artistic use of American money abroad has been the most salutary and gratefully received part of our money-aid. By what logic then can our government continue to ignore and even starve its arts at home? Shaw spoke of this matter in the England of 1890: "A fitter course would be to levy the cost [of orchestras] by the strong hand of the tax collector on the thousands of well-to-do people who never go to a concert because they are 'not musical,' but who enjoy, all the same, the health-giving atmosphere which music creates."

"Let's keep music out of politics," is the cry. Well, does anybody imagine that there are no politics in music now, or in the high patron-society that supports it? Surely, if we can trust our dollar-value to the Treasury, our dwindling natural resources to the Interior, our very survival to the State Department, we can afford to experiment with some sort of governmental aids—by grant if you will—to the art of music. What new cultural Sputnik will be needed to wake up this land to a realization that music deserves at least as much consideration as hog-husbandry and cheese-making?

What is most helpful about America is its innocence—that very quality that makes it the dupe of every alien musical cult, and that somehow prevents it from growing up to realize itself. But such innocence begins to look odd in a Herculean physique.

There is no predicting what we may become as an art nation. A people, like an individual, wishing to discover its talents, can only find the answer as a result of prolonged trials and labors. The conditions are bad, but the heart and spirit of the nation are good. We cannot all devote ourselves to a life of reform.

Let the private patron with his more modest means try in another direction then, perhaps even a selfish one. Let him leave the care of the large institutions to the foundations and the public purse, at the same time forcing his government to assume its proper obligations toward their support. Let him trust more his personal inclinations, and demand that he receive for his philanthropies a genuine return in entertainment, gratitude, and above all artistic satisfaction. Let him endow and commission *individual artists*, with the expectation of acknowledgment through dedication. Let him create opportunity for talents already trained, rather than glut the market with a superfluity of new trainees beyond what the present schools provide. The mistakes born of personal taste will probably be smaller than those born of an altruism cloaked in institutions. It is better he serve a few well than a great number badly. "In the great period of the Renaissance," said Whitehead, "the princes bought pictures that were being painted then, not centuries before."

The Price of Waste

While the motive of American economy today is profit, its method is waste. Waste has its critics, but they are soon silenced. A mere touch of economy at any one point of our political and business structure could bring the whole structure of industry down on our heads overnight, and who wants to risk that? That is why economy measures are looked on as slightly subversive. Waste is an old tradition, stemming from pioneering days, when every resource seemed inexhaustible. Its momentum goes on today, long after we've reached our geographic limits.

It now takes two tons of steel and three hundred horsepower to move a hundred pounds of female humanity down the street to attend a sale of hosiery; to announce which a full page advertisement is put in the paper; to fashion which a corps of experts is hired; to train which special college courses are cooked up; to pay for which, and sundry academic luxuries, we all must pay extra taxes; to pay which we borrow from the bank; to secure the loan for which we mortgage our house. It turns out to be an expensive bargain.

How few of our labors are really essential today?

Waste invades all quarters. No law restrains the farmer from ruining his land *for all time* by overgrazing, with subsequent ero-

148

sion. No law hinders another man from dredging over a Colorado valley for a little useless gold, and leaving behind a permanent wilderness of upturned boulders. No law prevents a man darkening the sky with factory smoke, where oranges once grew. This man may not steal my purse, but he may rob me of the sun: indeed, he is praised for it since he "creates employment." No law protects the streets, the lawns, the stately homes, the gardens, the elms and maples, the dignities and tranquilities of ten thousand villages from the invasion of freight trucks—those roaring and spitting new thirty-ton monsters. No franchise was needed. The trucks just took possession, aided and abetted and paid for by the victims, the taxpayers.

Even the new and ever more abundant leisure is drawn into the cycle of waste. For leisure is patterned more and more after labor; while labor gets to look more and more like leisure. Not that labor is becoming pleasanter. It only becomes softer and more monotonous, as indeed leisure does. One day the two will be scarcely distinguishable; just as in music concord and discord have become intertwined and inseparable. Recreation is now a major business, run on the same principles as industry. It studies how to relieve us of the new tediums it has just created. Talking, walking, silence, solitude, contemplation, simple handwork, pure idleness, all the old offspring of leisure have been made fearsome, alongside the tempos created by the instruments of distraction. So many new vacuums must be filled, and effortlessly filled at that. There must be no more manual or mental labor in the process. The remotest vacation lands are circumscribed with the familiar round of sports and distractions: a place without golfing, bathing girls, fishing, and television is not to be endured. Presently we will advertise the Himalayas in these proven terms, and the passenger plane that carries us there without benefit of swimming pool will be obsolete.

Now we come to music, the use of which, to supply the insatiable demand of radio (that must be fed twenty solid hours of the day) is the most riotously wasted of all our resources. It is, of course, a resource, though man-made. Are not all of our resources, in a sense, man-made? Their very discovery, all that led to their being sought out, and all the ingenuity that led to their use are a product of man. Our classical music is an inherited wealth, like our paintings, churches, temples, and our poetry. It is the distillation of the most sensitive thought, the purest devotion, the intensest passion, the loftiest aspiration of centuries of great men of genius.

Does it cost nothing to use this wastefully? It is like a man's labor. No labor at all makes for sloth; sufficient labor makes for health; and too much labor makes for exhaustion. The classics, if you will allow the comparison, need exercise and use; but they will soon die from over-use and exhaustion at the present rate. It is bad enough to din trivial music into our ears all day long. It is worse to use the masterpieces for this purpose. They will tell you how the radio has caused millions to know the *Unfinished* and the *Eroica* symphonies. But how *do* they know them? Mostly as dinner music, music to which to talk, argue, buy, sell, or read newspapers. In short, as "entertainment." But these works were never meant to be entertainment. Do you bring your newspapers, your radio, your business deals, your dinners into church? I do not say all good music is religious, but a great deal more of it is than is commonly recognized. Most fine music is a prayer, "the soliloquy of a jubilant soul," in Emerson's words. Or else it is, as Lanier said, "love in search of a word." "Music comes eons before religion," said Whitehead. "If the king loves music," said Mencius, "it is well with the land." "Music," said Beethoven, "is a higher revelation than philosophy." "Bach," said Dr. Schweitzer, "includes religion in the definition of art in general; all great art, even secular, is religious in his eyes." In any event, music is not to be used indiscriminately, wastefully, carelessly, or for the purpose of selling something. Waste music and you waste men's souls.

As a calling, is there another profession that wastes its trainees like this one? Every year thousands of men and women, trained in their diverse musical specialities, leave our colleges and conservatories looking for something to do. The professional world of music, operating solely out of New York, has no place for them. Stars alone are its business, and business alone is its guiding star. All this young talent will find asylum in teaching only; will further multiply the ranks of this most ephemeral of all professions; and carry on the traditional fiction of hope, again multiplying its own waste. Talent will wither and rot in all quarters. Meanwhile "music" is reputed to be the fifth or sixth largest industry in the country with outlays running into ten figures.

You are paid in music to be *not* a musician. You are trained for a non-profession. You are lured into it by a lie. You are taxed to support a futility. Is this not a waste?

And yet, every instinct and precept of the artist, particularly the musician, is against waste. His creed is economy. The whole art of counterpoint teaches how to make the most out of the least. Never was a richer use made of the slenderest means than did Bach in *The Well-tempered Clavichord*. This work has become known as music's Bible. In it are perfectly wedded, poetry and ingenuity; gravity and simplicity; fullness and economy. Music goes far afield in grandeur and opulence, but its substructure remains this same simplicity and even penury of means. Paraphrasing Thoreau, one could say, it is rich in proportion to the number of things it can afford to let alone.

Well, what does waste matter, if the real talent comes through? "Genius will have its say," we reassure ourselves bravely, denying the possibility of the forever derelict masterpiece. When Mark Twain's Captain Stormfield thought to find Shakespeare in Heaven, it took him a long time, for there were so many souls esteemed higher in dramatic genius by heavenly standards, but who had never become known on earth, having never had the chance. Some artists "can take it," others not. There are the vigorous men like Michelangelo, Rubens, Handel, Beethoven, or Shaw, who will not be put down; who insist on being heard and seen. But there are also the men of fragile temperament like

Schubert, Chopin, Keats, Poe, Cezanne, and Van Gogh, who are easily bent or broken under the conditions of life. Is genius then to be rewarded only when it is aggressive?

Art has never been fully at home anywhere. Perhaps in Bali music may be as nearly domesticated as possible. Perhaps in Pericles' Athens and the Medici's Florence the visual arts "belonged," enjoyed what we could call citizen rights. Even Beethoven's Vienna treated two of its greatest sons, Mozart and Schubert, like stepchildren. In America, half of its great have gone through life unknown and unrewarded. In posthumity, we can safely say, we take second place to none.

Perhaps the price of political democracy is democracy in the arts.

It is not the ugliness of cities that hinders the artist. Beauty has a way of invading every nook of the earth that is open to the sun, the wind, and the human eye. But there is one way that it can be killed and that is to allow it to be smothered in surfeit and vulgarity. Today the eye meets the travesties of art at every turn of the road; the ear is everywhere wearied by nauseous effigies of music. Doubtless the wear on the nerves will one day be measured statistically; then we may expect remedies, the physical body being ever our first concern.

Of all the senses, hearing has been the most abused in our time. To the horrors of war, technology has now added the special horrors of peace, the more insidious for their power of attraction.

Unfortunately, while you can close your eyes, you have not been given the means to close your ears.

The musician, who should be alive to the tones of life and nature, must suspend his principal sense, or else lay himself open to violent and nauseous sounds that are as unnecessary as they are inescapable. From noise he can expect no quarter. And of all noises, organized noise is the worst, the noise with intention, the noise he cannot ignore, either in ear or mind.

"There are people who smile at such things," said Schopenhauer in a day long before man discovered the electrical magnification of sound, "because they are insensitive to noise. . . . We have to do with pure wantonness, nay, with an impudent defiance offered to those members of the community who work with their heads. . . . A man's body and its needs are now everywhere treated with tender indulgence. . . . Is a thinking mind then to be the only thing that is never to obtain the slightest measure of consideration or protection, to say nothing of respect?"

If you are housed close to anyone else, as most of us are, you can count no moment secure from your neighbor's radio. The baritone announcer invades your study and bedroom at all hours. No law protects your privacy. But your neighbor, having invested in the flourishing business of noise-machinery, is secure in his thoughtless disregard of your peace of mind.

If you hope for a quiet Sunday in the country, you find that every motorcyclist, flier and hot-rodder is celebrating this day of rest with sounds like a dentist's drill.

If you camp in the wilds, the forest notes are likely to be the marshmallow chords of crooners, by which the neighboring camp is provided with a comforting assurance of safer urban propinquities.

If you live near an airport, your parlor at times would seem to house an ore-crusher.

A lake—any lake—on a summer evening, becomes a raging nest of outboard hornets.

You renounce the water and retire to your backyard, only to discover that latest internal-combustion scourge, your neighbor's power mower.

You then retire to the privacy of your house. But a new voice invades it—the sound truck. You lay down your work in resignation, a captive to some college prankster.

If you work in a store, your labors are insidiously lubricated with Musak. As you walk down the street, the *Jupiter Symphony* cackles obscenely out of some radio shop.

Is there a restaurant where conversation can sustain itself against the lachrymose droolings of a love-sick juke box?

You may think there remain some "wilderness areas" that are

safe. But the mockingbird that you had hoped would awaken you at dawn proves to be a power saw, perhaps miles away, retching out some tune of progress.

Silence now is an abhorred fugitive. "Sound itself," remarks Gide, "so gradually and exquisitely liberated from noise, is now returning to it." Can anyone imagine Wordsworth, Beethoven, Whitman, Thoreau, Emerson, Brahms (all of them great walkers) conceiving their art under such conditions?

It is no wonder, in the face of such an assault on the ears, that sensitive music goes into hiding, or that composers retreat into the monastic seclusion of the recondite, and give us surrealistic tonal-arithmetic instead of song.

And so music needs its special preserves, if it is to survive. Like the Indians, it is given reservations wherein it may recover some of the leisure and reflection of which it has been robbed by the precipitate modern world. Philanthropy has been generous with prizes, commissions, colonies, grants-in-aid, ivory towers, foundations, Fulbrights and fellowships. Never before has the musician had so many aids. But are these not perhaps a substitute for outlets of a more normal kind? They can be likened to our National Parks, which were established to save a few salient features of nature from the exploitation we call "improvement." Europe, far more densely populated than America, full as any continent with natural beauties, has had little need for such national parks. For it has been obliged to conserve its resources from ancient times. The greatest wars in history have been fought in Europe. Yet the scars these have left are as nothing beside the mutilations of our landscape, all very recent: the erosions all through our South, the rubble of California's mountain valleys, the blackened Oregon forests, the dustbowls, the bulldozed hills, the auto graveyards, the fields ruined with needless or obsolete pavements. And the cities themselves, how unutterably dreary. Are they not wastelands, more than any desert? H. L. Mencken remarked, "I have seen, I believe, all the most unlovely towns of the world; they are all to be found in the United States. . . . Here is something that the psychologists have so far neglected, the love of ugliness for its own sake, the lust to make the world intolerable. Its habitat is the United States. . . . The etiology of this madness deserves a great deal more study than it has got."

Abroad, who speaks of conservation? Every peasant practices it. Switzerland, Holland, Austria, Denmark, France, Scandinavia —they are all virtually national parks in themselves, preserved not by forest rangers, but by the people.

And so it is in the arts. We would not need such sheltering for artists, if we granted them normal citizen rights, the same protection as industry, the same subsidies, the same voice in government. *The arts need to have a home to be at home:* a place of nourishment and love. But a marriage like this must be mutual and based on respect. "Beauty," said Emerson, "must come back to the useful arts. The distinction between the fine and the useful arts must be forgotten." The Muse needs not pampering, but respecting.

Is there no time for beauty? Are we still too busy getting settled? We have put it off long already; yet every day it seems farther away. This moral waste, this germ of restlessness that infects us the very moment we arrive at a point of rest, the human installments we pay to achieve an overnight obsolescence! Build yourself a place of beauty, and tomorrow the surveyors are out there plotting a six-lane highway. With no by-your-leave they will bulldoze your hard-won domestic creation, or insult your view, and fill the air with foul sounds. The agents of waste have again found you out. You are not to complain. For the new road will carry you countryward safer, quicker, farther. You can build another home on the sale of your old, and enjoy it during the next hectic installment of your nomadic life. That's the approved way. Your taxes support it.

Where shall we begin then to remedy this waste, if indeed it can be remedied? In music the first step will be to overcome its own constipation, until a measure of real hunger again develops. No taste without hunger. After that, moderation. I propose, unless better measures are devised, that *all music used for advertis-*

ing be taxed, on a graded scale, the old works as well as the new ones carrying performing rights. If the government can tax us for things we need, like soap, razor blades, gasoline, and earnings, it ought all the more to tax us for things we do not need. Advertising, on its present scale, takes second place to nothing as a superfluity. And its consort is music.

The ear will have to be thirsted again no less than satisfied. No man will be obliged to hear music unwillingly, unless, indeed, music is to be used as a form of punishment in our penal institutions. In fact, all unnecessary noises are to be curbed in the same way we now are beginning to curb the smoke nuisance. The art of music will be restored to its befitting dignity.

The native musician will learn to be self-reliant. Every region is to have its full-rounded, autonomous music center. The artist is to be taken from the periphery back to the center, and the huckster from the center back to the periphery. The artist will have his place beside the lawyer, teacher, doctor, craftsman, in government and in society.

"The American compact" says Whitman, "is altogether with individuals. . . . The whole theory of the universe is directed unerringly to one single individual—namely to You."

Changing Concepts

Every art is subject to the principle, familiar enough in other walks of life, that *gains entail losses*. It is true that today our knowledge of music's history and literature embraces a wider span of years than in, say, the days of Schubert, who could not possibly have known the Elizabethan music, nor heard a single strain from the Far East, nor even traced the Gregorian Chant as far back as our scholars of today have done. Communication, publication, the issuance of records, and the immense accretion of material in libraries: all these have helped to allow the observer of today to view the geography of music as if he saw great portions of the land from a high-flying plane. Where once he floated down a narrow stream, walled in by its banks and skimming over the graveled stream bed below, he now takes in the entire course of the river as on a map, yet has lost meanwhile the poetry of detail. The spire of rock he once took two hazardous days to climb, is now but a red tack sticking out of the ochre desert below. The great canyon with its roaring precipitate river is now but a wound in the landscape, a gully with a delicate ribbon of green and white running through. But if we wish to adventure like him, we have no choice but to come down out of the sky once more and take up the ancient labors and discomforts of primitive travel. For art has produced no air travel, has dis-

157

covered no technological shortcuts. Its creation needs another tempo than ours of today. The artist now wastes the greater part of his vitality in recovering the patience to plod once more at a rate appropriate to all great and enduring achieving.

It is hard for us to envision a time when melody was not corralled in our present scales. Not that the simple intervals of the fifth, the fourth, the third, and the second did not predominate as now; but there was every liberty in the free use of these. Melody was closer to speech, and its inflections were not confined to precise intervals as today. What to us would be an aberration of pitch was then an allowable means of expression. Likewise its rhythms were not limited to our time units, which are mostly but multiples of two, sometimes three.

With the development of harmony and counterpoint, following the unharmonized plain song, and folk song, there were gradually established fixed scales (or modes) and fixed time values. With this momentous change, melody began to lose its freedom in interval and time. But eventually the loss brought about a gain. The later fixed scale-notes and exact time units made possible, like the rectilinear concepts of building in architecture, the construction of larger musical edifices than had ever been possible before. Further dimension was added, with harmony and polyphony. With the later adoption, then, of a tempered scale, and the chromaticism and modulation it invited, music achieved in time the vast cathedral-like monuments of Bach and Handel. Later again, with the further development of instruments came a new flexibility in range and tempo, leading through the "classic" era to the orchestral monuments of Wagner, Tschaikovsky, Strauss and the "moderns." Meanwhile the purity of an older vocal style had gradually to be sacrificed for these recent instrumental triumphs. There is always a tendency to exploit the more recently developed techniques to their final inconsiderate limits. Restraint or moderation operate no more in music than in building. The grandest old mansions are often the first to fall before the mediocre houses of the moment. Bach himself fell a victim to the new operatic fashions of his day. Now, despite our technology we have almost come about to the end of experimentation with the "classical" instruments; the technique of dissonance has preoccupied musical writers, causing them to feel ill at ease in the use of a musical speech considered grammatical a generation earlier.

Not to belittle the achievements of moderns, there is nevertheless something deceptive about carrying to farther and farther extremes a particular element such as dissonance—something that defeats the very ends that are sought. The defiant, dissentient, or crabbed quality of discord loses itself in an unrelieved succession of such sounds. Beyond limits, dissonance is no longer perceived dissonantly.

Thus, atonality, the last step in the avoidance of the consonant, instead of producing a striking effect, tends rather to reduce the hearer to a state of tonal amnesia. Its contrapuntal niceties, its inversions, retrograde movements, and so forth, are impossible to apprehend, except if seen on the page. More credit is due to its celebrated author (who disclaimed the name of the system credited to him, and whose total musical achievements are withal impressive—not forgetting, as Shaw remarked, that, "Schönberg exhausted the fun of this and relapsed more and more into tonality"), than to his followers, some of whom would give the impression that they possess the exclusive key to the art of the future. In their evangelism, they remind one not a little of the class-struggle zealots of the Thirties. They would gladly strip music of ancient and established symbols, and give us, instead, a sterner catechism for the regeneration of sound. To the noninitiates this sometimes looks more like a leveling process which, stripping notes of their relative tonal rank and distinction, disposes them then along newly devised lines of lucubration. ("You don't need to employ atonality," Strauss is said to have remarked once to Hindemith, "for you have talent.") One has the impression that *promised new freedoms have eventuated in new and greater restrictions.*

It is laid upon our conscience that we must educate our ears to all such sounds. The listener's pleasure is not consulted in the matter, though it would seem that anyone paying admission to a concert ought to have the right to hear what attracts him rather than be victimized with the devices of aural mortification. The sensitive ear has been conscientiously dulled through a sort of aesthetic brainwash to the point of accepting anything. Naturally, the refinements of our older musical speech must suffer deprecia-tion as a consequence. *Music has gained tolerance and lost sapience.* Says Robert Frost, "Then there is the wildness whereof it is spoken. Our problem then is, as modern abstractionists, to have the wildness pure; to be wild when there is nothing to be wild about."

Some of these attempts at artistic liberation remind one of a reform in chess. Let us suppose, in order to provide variety and novelty, the movements of the pieces were all to be changed; the queen demoted, the pawns promoted, the castles and bishops routed along new courses; the whole board shorn of its tradition. Doubtless a new form of game would be possible. But will any-one succeed in inventing moves that are more perfectly con-ceived to exploit the geometrical face of the checkered board than the old ones? And who will presume to declare the old game antiquated and exhausted, after centuries of the same rules?

An art, like a game, can only move within its rules. *Without limits, it has also no objectives;* and without objectives there is no movement; lacking movement it becomes static; being static it has no life.

In a spirit of appeasement, it is often said that a great inte-grating mind will presently fuse all these present experiments and confusions into some great new organic art. But who knows whether a future generation may not look on our present re-searches and anarchies as a catalogue of errors, and simply ignore or reject them, as we have rejected numerous hypotheses in medicine or physics with each later discovery of their insuffi-ciency. The error lies in assuming that the tendencies of the moment will indefinitely persist graph-wise. Need an aesthetic curve persist in its present course any more than the index of a certain security on the stock market? Shall we disregard the possibility of fluctuations, reversals, revolutions, the tidal changes in the arts as of the past?

The atonalists are so numerous now that they have tilted the scales so that persons retaining a respect for tradition suddenly discover themselves to be the heretics, the radicals; while the erstwhile radicals have become the conformists who, even had they the gift to be simple, would deny themselves the courage to exercise it, such is the force of the aesthetic prohibition.

"Language," says Tovey, "is not extended by declining to use what is known of it." The inability of a composer to invest a triad with new imaginative meaning is not necessarily a mark of distinction. Rather it may point to a poverty of resource. Surely, modern life is not lacking in new material for the artist. The literary writer does not find grammatical language unsuitable for contemporary expression. Must the painter than jettison his perspective, flaunt his contrived misproportions, and engage himself in a contest to determine who can achieve the ultimate aberration, in order to prove himself modern and original? Must the composer bend his entire efforts toward *the avoidance of all he has inherited,* throw out harmony like an old shoe, and then, having achieved anarchy and destroyed all respect for his more immediate artistic parentage, pose with perverse respectability as a worshipper of Lassus and Bach?

Of these composers, who like to talk of the common man and of humanity, yet who join themselves at once to an international circle promulgating this loftiest of intellectual snobberies, one could say with Yeats: "The best lack all conviction, while the worst are full of passionate intensity."

D. C. al Fine

BRIEFLY SAID

I should have liked to produce a good book. This has not come about, but the time is past in which I could improve it.

LUDWIG WITTGENSTEIN

The Performer

"One must *be* something in order to *do* anything," said Goethe; to which it should be added that only in *doing* something will one ever *become* something.

Art has few shortcuts. The way to make effort effortless is to practice effort.

The inferior interpreter relegates as much of his thought and emotion as possible to the unconscious and the automatic. The superior interpreter lifts these up to the highest appropriate level of awareness. The one seeks security, the other strives for intensity.

The problem in learning a new work is to retain the initial feelings it inspires during the long labors and repetitions required for its mastery. This calls for an astute rationing of emotion, indeed, a certain cold-bloodedness in the working out of technical detail. A man would be unwise to exhaust in its carpentry and plumbing the enthusiasm he feels for the ensemble of a noble tower he is building.

Truth in art means the honest revelation of the personality. This is not possible without skill. Yet the highest degree of skill, nay, virtuosity, while it implies a measure of bigness in the man, will not avail to conceal his essential littleness. By the same token, a limited virtuosity need not conceal a man's bigness. The immaturity of musical America shows itself in that we place virtuosity above all else, and make a fetish of "perfectionism."

Some people, because of their admiration for the austere purity of chamber music, have the idea that it is more difficult to play in a good quartet than to play solo. They forget how much stimulation comes from the interaction with fellow performers and how much responsibility lies with the soloist who, unaided, must hold an audience throughout an entire concert. The same is true as regards conducting, which is generally admired as the highest musical art of our times, when it is, in fact, apart from its organizational and tactful aspects, probably the least demanding.

Of all devices of expression, the vibrato is the most abused. One after the other, the orchestra's wind instruments have taken it over from the strings—the flute, the bassoon, the oboe, the trumpet, the trombone, and now the clarinet and the horn—forgetting that the older composers must have had in mind a contrast between the warmth of the strings and the coolness of the winds. If all play vibrato, where are the cool colors? For the vibrato *is* warmth. Not that the winds should be denied the expression of warmth, only that it should be used where it was so intended. Many players, including the strings as well, can no longer even play non-vibrato; and few cultivate the manifold gradations of vibrato, in amplitude as well as speed, from the least to the fullest. With many it is just slapped on the tone thoughtlessly and automatically, with a result almost as vulgar as is produced by the electric organ with its obscene ululation of the air, by means of its tremulant.

The artist truly worthy of his pay is the one who is amply paid already in the privilege of exercising his art, whether that is writing, conducting, concertizing, or even teaching, provided he has learners attuned to himself. Paul Horgan, the novelist and historian, once led the Dallas Symphony Orchestra through Schubert's *Unfinished Symphony* in a rehearsal, begging them beforehand to overlook any wrong directions he as an amateur might give. When he had finished, he sighed, "And to think people are paid to do this heavenly task."

The Critic

I do not expect to find in my time a great genius in music, but I will be content to find a great personality.

"My God," says the critic, "the man still talks about beauty. Doesn't he know the times have changed?"

Our music, like much of our youth today, leaps directly from naïveté to cynicism, enjoying little of happy maturing in between.

In music our most imposing monuments have been tombs for the living and dormitories for the dead.

Music, once the divinest of the graces, has now dressed itself in the neatly tailored suit of a "problem."

An excess of reputation is as bad for the famous as is its total absence for the neglected. The unjust disparity has always existed, but now it is limitlessly magnified through modern electronics and Madisonavenuism. The brighter the searchlight's beams, the blacker the night around it.

The finest tribute to the past is not to elevate it to a tyranny over the present.

A Some-one has always a different inflection and bearing than a No-one. Since in music there is scarcely ever a ladder of promotion from one extreme to the other, one seldom sees a man at either end who has learned to carry himself with ease.

The original musicians of America are like sticks of firewood, scattered so widely they can produce no flame, while in Manhattan they are piled so thick that any flame would suffocate from want of air.

The land of greatest opportunity is at once the home of greatest frustration. A beggar is twice beggared when turned away from his own prosperous threshold.

In this day when the schizophrenic world threatens suicide, when we shoot to the moon and the stars, when we keep pace with the setting sun, when the Orient sows its oats and Africa gives a mighty waking yawn, shall we take time out to count the notes of a tone row to make sure all twelve are there, or shall we write learned tomes on a painter's doodle?

In Italy a musical failure calls forth hisses and catcalls. In Russia, I'm told, it evokes an arctic silence. In America only the experienced ear can distinguish between the applause that greets success and the applause that soothes failure. The reason for this is not lack of musicality, nor an excess of courtesy; rather it is unconviction, an immature eclecticism, or else a self-conscious fear of making a mistake. If this is a fault, it may yet prove to be a lesser one than Europe's hardened certainties.

To fire, or be fired by, others is always easier than to fire yourself alone (perhaps in an imaginary consanguinity), just as solitaire is a last resort in the absence of partners for bridge.

I have a high regard for the man who has pioneered alone and unaided in art. Shall I measure him with the yardstick of Athens, Florence, and Vienna? Must I balance MacDowell with Brahms, Audubon with Leonardo, Hawthorne with Goethe? Stone Mountain, rising some hundreds of feet out of the eroded flats of Georgia, has moved me no less than Mount Whitney, scarcely distinguishable from its fourteen-thousand-foot neighbors.

They say a critic writes when he cannot *do*. However much this needs qualification, one should ask whether one who *does* would do well to write criticism. For to be at once in the arena and in the referee's box is apt to cancel out the impulse of both. A man's judgment will suffer from the vulnerability of his creations, while his creations will suffer from the catholicity needed for judgment.

As between truth and tact, which should a critic choose? Tact can be weakness and insipidity, while truth can be arrogance and injuriousness; and then too, where is the *absolute* in artistic truth? Both praise and blame, when they are too generously and continuously bestowed, lose their force and become tiresome. Certain it is that the superior critic *is* something; is an artist of judgment no less than a judge of artists.

The Author

There is more first-rateness in being honestly your second-rate self than in being imitatively some first-rate other.

How lucky that the "classic" composers did not know that they were "classical." How unlucky that the "moderns" cannot forget they are "moderns."

As only the mother knows what childbirth really is, so it is only the creator of art who knows its labor pains. The musicologist can talk about music's embryology, but he has never yet laid an egg.

Music feeds no less on indignation, despair, and grief than it does on love, ecstasy, and fulfillment. But the dinner, once begun, is satisfying regardless. Indeed, to sing of sorrow is art's greatest joy of all.

The artist of today tends to reason himself out of doing, talk himself out of tasting, read himself out of seeing and secure himself out of all high adventure.

More art results from the need to escape suffering than from the desire to express it.

An art, like wine, may need aging, but left too long untended it sometimes turns to vinegar.

Whoever has not been despised and rejected will never understand what this means, nor will the seed of resistance ever bear fruit in him; and he will lack something—a moral vitamin, perhaps. "Rejection makes strong," said Frederick Stock to a composer, in variation of the old German saw that "whatever fails to kill, strengthens." He might have added that acceptance kindles the heart, and indeed he was of all conductors here perhaps the most hospitable to native and regional music.

An artist, like a mother, is intent on his latest offspring. The product of a lifetime covered with the dust of a week's neglect he will sacrifice, rather than the product of his last hour.

The only proper self-expression is self-obliteration. Because a man is a spring, he is not therefore the author of water.

For the artist the barest scrap of his own creation is a reprieve from the hard facts of life. For this reason, once he has tasted creation, he is committed to its labors for the rest of his days, whether they yield him success or not.

The world is interested less in an artist's originality than in his personality. Originality is the scholar's esoteric fruit, to be savored without the responsibility of producing it. It eludes those who seek to create it with intention. It comes, if at all, unbidden to the honest workman in his labors of discipline and self-search.

I have a great deal of faith in American art; for as fast as one generation is corrupted with frustration, the next is on its way, bubbling with hope; and I notice that all the efforts of the former to instruct the latter, through its experience, prove futile.

There was a time when the composer, however famous, lent himself willingly to serve the interpreter. Today the interpreter makes it a point of honor to serve the composer; an odd anomaly at a time when the virtuoso so far outranks the composer in emolument and social esteem.

The Teacher

Teaching is an intellectual parenthood; your debt to the past is best paid to the future.

The peril of a teacher is that he inclines to reveal all his secrets. Once the last secret has fled, what remains? He is stripped to a pitiful nudity, the while his clothes are shredded for paint-rags.

Personalities, like liquids, seek their own level. The period of a wave depends on the depth of water, and between two waves born of unequal depth the one may destroy the other through an unsympathetic rhythm. Thus between student and teacher there must be an attunement. To discover this should be, and seldom is, the concern of an administrator.

Learning has three stages: imitation, growth, and the achievement of freedom. Through each of these the learner's dependence should steadily lessen. In the end, better independent imperfection than dependent perfection. Some teachers make chronic musical invalids of their students, causing them to need "lessons" all through life. The superior teacher sends his pupils away with his blessing when they have found their wings.

You cannot teach a man anything he does not already know. Technicalities, yes, but not the things that really matter in an art. The best lesson takes place when the teacher formulates that which is already there in the student, latent but unformed. The student says to himself, "Now, why didn't I think of that without being told?" But he feels a rightful claim to it, nevertheless, having already possessed what needed only to be articulated.

It is not the principles of music a young writer must learn, but rather the principles of his own course of action which is hammered out through long labors and a careful study of his likes and dislikes. He looks not for rules, but for his own direction.

Until someone invents a test for desire and aspiration, *all the tests for musical talent will prove useless*. Talent is the rule and not the exception. In excess it is often wasted, while a small amount of it may be nursed into something very fine; and beauty is not to be appraised by size.

The decline of a school begins when procedure takes precedence over accomplishment. The decline of its teaching shows when method supersedes matter.

Every college music catalog is now stuffed with courses which carry high-sounding descriptions and stern qualifications as to eligibility, as if music were a cumulative science like mathematics wherein each level of learning depended strictly on the mastery of another. Quite often the fanciest courses listed are nothing but window-dressing, and seldom if ever given. Many schools even see no need to mention who is the instructor, as if this were of no importance, or were a matter to be entrusted solely to a benevolent administration. Considering the cost of college instruction and the vulnerability of talent (I could almost say, the greater the talent, the greater the vulnerability), it would seem that the greatest emphasis should be placed on *who* teaches or directs. The teacher is paramount and the course quite secondary.

In administration, the man who is selfless enough to surround himself with others greater than himself is even rarer than the man who is great enough to fear no rivals.

It is interesting that the professor has steadily lost stature at the very time that he has come to participate more fully in committees, senates, and appointments. This is due in part to his relative fiscal decline, and the growing disparity of income between teachers and administrators. But a better reason for this may be found in the readiness of administrators to fill vacancies with obscure young persons who may be engaged at low cost, and who are ready to fit into a preconceived pattern. This results in averageness or often mediocrity which perpetuates itself by virtue of what is proudly described as a faithful regimen of democracy. At any rate, the modern way is to fit the man into the course rather than build the course around the man.

A school reducing its enrollment through choice rather than necessity would be a refreshing novelty in these days when achievement is measured in numbers.

A man's duties should not be measured so much in time as in preoccupation. This is why a creative man will hesitate before taking on administration, which requires that his thoughts be full of people instead of sounds, colors, and things of the imagination. Nevertheless, it would be a blessing to the arts if administration, even for a limited time, were imposed as a social duty on the best creative men, rather than solicited as a stepping-stone by career men. For power is safest in the hands of those who seek it not; and institutional enterprise is best assured under those who have demonstrated enterprise on their own.

It is interesting that while modern American education offers learning to children in the guise of entertainment, it offers what should be entertainment to adults in the guise of learning. For the higher learning in the arts *is* entertainment: opera, theatre, concerts, and books. For the young, education makes play of learning; for the old, it makes learning of play. More money is spent here in teaching Sophocles, Shakespeare, Corneille, Goethe, Ibsen, Gluck, Mozart, Wagner, Verdi and Strauss in the classroom than is spent abroad in performing these same in the theatre, where they properly belong. Is this a lingering Puritanism that accredits pleasurable learning only when seasoned with laboriousness? Or have our pedants, like the turtle, won the race over the hare to the centers of academic legislation?

In a nation dominated by business and where the measure of a man is his income, the professor sits low in the social scale. His income is mostly years behind a relentless inflation, although in depression years his steady small salary (it's hard to kill a college) sometimes briefly becomes trumps. He is a confirmed borrower. His tenure makes him a sound risk; his indigence, a steady customer of the bank. More and more of his time goes to juggling his fiscal arrears. He finds he must pay ever more for his inability to pay (a valuable economic and sociological lesson, linking him, if loosely, to the vast community of those suffering need—but hardly worth its own price). To restore him in his proper place, society will have to pay him more in order that he may make himself worthy again of more pay. It will have to invest him with more dignity, so that he may be allowed to recover his own dignity.

Music and Society

Unlike Gaul, musical America is divided into two parts: Manhattan Island and whatever remains. Yet through it all runs a unifying idea: Manhattan believes it possesses everything of consequence, and in this the provinces appear to concur.

The veneration of a great man of former times is proper; but a veneration carried to extremes is a mark of contempt for the living, and is sufficient proof that he too would share in this contempt, were he alive.

Labor today takes the stand that, because the lowest tasks are the least pleasant, they should therefore receive the highest payment. Thus, as an artist, I must work three hours to pay for one hour's labor by one who cleans my sewer, or moves my piano. In this ratio I cannot fail to read society's measure of esteem.

Mr. Ford thought he was bringing the country closer to the average man's doorstep with his Model T. Mr. Edison doubtless thought the same as regards music with his phonograph. Does

178

the accessibility of music make us more musical? Is the country nearer now than in Beethoven's day?

I do not object to the clerk in music. But I object to the clerk who, by virtue of his rise to power through business and administration, assumes power over the artist and makes a clerk of the artist.

The trick nowadays is to proletarianate an artistic idea, make it common currency, cause it to lose all pride of distinction. So the artist, who from time immemorial has been the intellectual aristocrat, must now, like Coriolanus, exhibit his scars of battle, flatter every potential heckler, kiss every infant brat, and drink from the mob mug. And, like Coriolanus, he is sometimes driven to betray his own city.

In matters of public taste, no less than with the individual, it should be noted that just as liking something is conducive to doing it well, so also is doing it well conducive to liking it. No public polls are needed to establish the worth of mathematics. We teach it first of all, and then let come what will.

America has need of a new art, the art of leaving well-enough alone. Every wilderness now must be improved, civilized, made in the image of business; and so art too loses touch with Nature; and meeting her only at second hand, turns its back on her in contempt.

There is no freedom, once it is enthroned, that does not in its turn become a prohibition. In the arts it is the same.

We schedule our labors so man cannot partake of the light of the sun; and then we wonder that he has no eye for color, nor, for that matter, ear for the music of nature.

The captive audience: formerly in the preplumbing age it was the nose that was assaulted, now it is the ear, by this modern aural stench, Musak and all its cousins and its aunts. But it should be remembered that the one was unavoidable, the other is deliberate.

Hard as it is for littleness to conceive greatness, it is no less hard for greatness to conceive littleness. Since neither one has grown out of the other, and both are but realizations of their own latent selves, there is no recollection in either to enlighten on the point of view of the other.

As against the usual apology that we are too young a nation to have arrived at the full flowering of the arts, these words of John Adams, written during the dangerous deliberations leading to the Declaration of Independence: "I must study politics and war that my sons may have liberty to study mathematics and philosophy . . . in order to give their children a right to study painting, poetry and music."

Behind all our warring politics is the harmonizing unity of the grandfather principle in our Declaration and Constitution, neither of which possesses a thought not voiced a hundred times before, but glowing with personality born of a great purpose. In our music there is no such grandfather, and we drift around unrooted, unrelated, in multiple contentious bastardy.

What is American? This is as difficult to describe as to delineate a face in words. I only know it is easy to spot an American in Paris, Vienna, Rome, or London by his very gait. He grows out of our life here, its food, climate, politics, athletics, business, education, and all the rest. And so will our American music bear the earmarks of all these native elements, earmarks impossible to define, yet easy to distinguish. Looking around at our orchestras and operas, I do not find fault with their standards, but I know they are not American. Either we are artistically unworthy of them, or they are politically unworthy of us.

The patron should learn that to give wisely is as hard as to acquire shrewdly; to give unwisely is worse than to give not at all. The artist has no less responsibility in making worthy use of patron benefaction, and must learn to accept this with proper spirit and gratitude. Nowadays when giver and receiver rarely meet, what with all the middlemen between, the transaction can easily deteriorate and become casual, thoughtless, graceless, and even devious and political.

Jefferson thought popular government the best means to assure the leadership of the "natural aristoi," as against the hereditary rule of kings and princes. Democracy was to him a leveling of *opportunity* and not of *talent;* it was never meant as an invitation to a rule of averageness and mediocrity. The art of music is subject to the same possibilities; but through the active performance of its classics, the aristocratic ideal of *personality* has been kept alive. Thus music continues to sing of ecstasy, reverence, grandeur and lovingness, most of which have been lost to the church, first in its resistance to an inevitable science, later in its all-too-hasty leap onto the bandwagon of materialist modernity. Music, having retained many of these traits, could re-inspirit our politics, which too have sagged in the wake of easy prosperity and consequent vulgarity. An art can passively reflect its times, or it can actively mold its times. A Beethoven is almost inconceivable today. Between him and the present age, one or the other would have to give way.

To the freedoms enumerated so often, and more particularly by President Franklin Roosevelt, let us add one or two more, the need for which has been occasioned by the very realization of some others. While fewer people in the United States today suffer hunger, joblessness, and curtailment of private opinion than at certain other periods, more and more feel the encroachments of modern life on their privacy, their enjoyment of silence, their communication with natural beauty, their investment in a suitable place to live secure from the ravages of sudden change, their right to express dissenting opinions beyond private conversation—and a few more. No man is more harassed today than is the composer, who often finds himself a hunted creature, for the most remorseless assault of our times on the senses is through the ear. He should, of course, be mindful of his own capacity to create a disturbance. Likewise, others should be mindful of his vulnerability to noises and more particularly to unwanted music. For he cannot possibly think his own sounds while hearing others.

Once a year the carpetbagger from the Big City moves into our town, gathers up all its loose musical monies and promises to deliver in exchange a neat package of next season's concerts. As a business venture, his plan is sound, since it leaves no debts behind. But as a musical policy, it ties up all local enterprises with a shoe-string. More thoroughly than in baseball, the Big Leagues have swallowed up the minor leagues and just about everything else. At the very moment when the major cities of America have reached a maturity and self-sufficiency comparable to the large centers abroad, which should entitle them to the fullest measure of regional autonomy, they are sapped of enterprise and subdued to a state of musical vassalage and spiritual impotence. How is it with a nation bursting with talent and drooping in opportunity? A generation ago every large center served its area with excellent moderately paid artists. Today our immeasurably more developed land is served by a handful of over-paid, over-advertised, over-privileged (also over-worked, over-exploited, and over-taxed) artists, who have indeed no choice but to accept the all-or-nothing terms offered them by what could be described in the old sense as a musical House of Morgan.

You are not allowed in the arts to bring criticism in one hand unless you bring ready solutions in the other. Is this not a sign of insecurity? You are not to unsettle this going concern with questions. "Negativism," they call it. And yet experience tells us that the most important problems are often those that remain unsolved. And so it is with the musical problems I have raised. I do not know their solution, nor do I know that things will be better, if and when the particular ills I have described no longer operate; for I am quite certain that new ills will supplant them, perhaps worse ones.

As for me, I know nothing more depressing than to live in this air of perfumed optimism. A few sharp questions would seem to me like a breath of fresh air. The affirmation we need so very much today may first require the removal of mountains of pretense and confusion. Of the disclosure of unpleasant truths, Dr. Johnson said, "It keeps mankind from despair." Asked how Harvard College was getting along, President Eliot once said, "Now that a spirit of pessimism prevails, we are making progress." The Man of Peace was known between sermons to have picked up a whip to drive certain usurers from the temple. "Negativism," they might have called it.

But there is a vitality and faith in America that cannot be matched in the older corners of Europe, and it is bound to lead to some kind of musical outpouring greater than any we have yet experienced. It will cause, or be caused by, some larger, indigenous artistic freedoms. There will doubtless be a patriotic note in it, maybe even some strategy. But in the end, the only proper strategy for art, as well as politics, today is humanity. The world has for some time been hearing America's political voice in the counterpoint of nations. To this should be added now the artistic voice in which, let us hope, there will be much of robust health, ingratiation, fervor, generosity, and timeless grandeur.